ORION PLAIN

C000049073

numerology

numerology

ANNE CHRISTIE

Previously published in 2005 as *Simply Numerology* by
Zambezi Publishing Limited, Devon, UK

This edition first published in Great Britain in 2017 by
Orion
The Orion Publishing Group Ltd
Carmelite House, 50 Victoria Embankment,
London, EC4Y 0DZ
An Hachette UK Company

1 3 5 7 9 10 8 6 4 2

Interior design by Kathryn Sky-Peck

A CIP catalogue record for this book is available
from the British Library.

Paperback ISBN: 978 1 4091 6973 4

eBook ISBN: 978 1 4091 6974 1

Printed and bound by CPI Group (UK), Ltd, Croydon, CR0 4YY

www.orionbooks.co.uk

"Numbers are the language of the universe."

—Pythagoras

Contents

About
Numerology

People have studied numerology for many thousands of years in order to understand themselves and to unravel the mysteries of the future in much the same way as they have used astrology. Just as the signs and symbols of astrology contain a universal language, numbers as well embody their own unique esoteric knowledge. Many early civilizations, such as the ancient Egyptians, the Hebrews, the Chaldeans, and the Hindus studied numbers as a science. Many people today believe that everything from the divine to the mundane hides in numbers, and that a person who understands the language of numbers can unlock their energies can discover their secrets.

Numerology has always had mystical and spiritual significance. The two main sources of our current systems of numerology are the Greek philosopher, mathematician, and astrologer, Pythagoras, and the Hebrew Kabbalah.

Sometimes called the Father of Numerology, Pythagoras (5th century BC) spent a lifetime studying numbers. He was convinced that numbers had mystical properties, and he defined the system of numerical classification that we still use today. In math, every schoolchild learns the Pythagorean Theorem, a fundamental property of geometry he formulated. Pythagoras believed that numbers contained the secrets of the entire universe; some of his ideas postulated that the most powerful (masculine) numbers were the

Pythagoras, the Father of Numerology

odd ones, while the even numbers were less powerful (and feminine). This universal concept also shows up in the I Ching, but Pythagoras would not have had contact with Chinese thinkers in those ancient days.

Moving forward in time to the early 16th century, we find the philosopher Henry Agrippa, who devised a system that relates man to numbers. In the 18th century, Count Cagliostro invented his own system of numerology that gave prophetic readings. Both these men based their systems on the ancient Kabbalistic system of *gematria*—a numerical system that was both mystic and revelatory.

Other students of the occult believed that when one transcribed the letters of a person's name into numbers, the results were similar to an astrological chart. One of the most famous numerologists of the 19th century was Count Louis Hamon, who we know by his assumed name of Cheiro. He was an astrologer, numerologist, and palmist; his sobriquet, "Cheiro," derives from the word *cheiromancy*, meaning "palmistry."

Many famous and influential clients consulted Cheiro, including King Edward VII.

This plain and simple book is meant to introduce you to the fascinating study of numerology, and give you some tools to understand yourself and others, and perhaps even have a peak at your destiny!

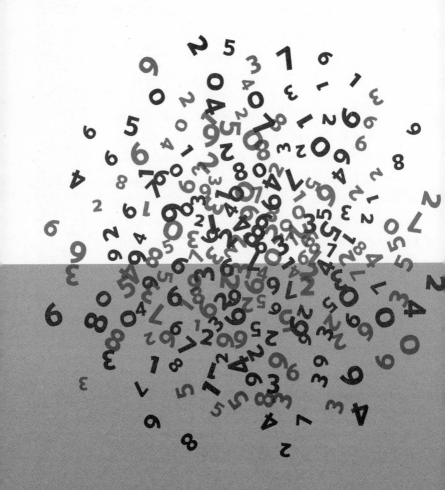

A Brief
History
of Numbers

1

Numbers are fascinating, with an ancient and rich history. Here is a very brief overview of that history, and how numbers have come to be used in numerology.

Language and Numbers

The earliest form of numbers came from Babylon and Mesopotamia, the fertile area around the Tigris and Euphrates rivers, the area which encompasses the country we now call Iraq. This area is often referred to the "cradle of civilization," for it is here that complex urban centers sprang up. Up to that time, humans lived a simple hunting or farming existence and they had no need to keep records. Cities brought the first forms of business and the subsequent need to account for animals that people bought and sold, and the need to account for the purchase and sale of grain and other goods. The earliest writing in this area was called *cuneiform*, dating back to 3500 BC; it was basically an enhanced bookkeeping system.

Egyptian writing (circa 3000 BC) and Chinese writing (circa 1500 BC) derived from pictograms (pictures) that eventually became connected to sounds or words. As time went by, the sounds and word meanings evolved; they gradually lost their pictorial form and drifted into looking like early forms of writing.

Letters as Numbers

Hebrew and Ancient Greek

An early type of writing that depended upon an actual alphabet was Hebrew. This is a language that, like most, has also gone through various incarnations over the millennia; however, it has not changed as much as many other forms of language. Aleph is still aleph and bet is still bet—although even within modern memory, there are people who have pronounced bet as *beth* or even *base*.

The Hebrews didn't have a separate number system, so they simply used the letters of the alphabet as numbers, such as

$$\aleph = 1 \quad \beth = 2 \quad \gimel = 3 \quad \daleth = 4$$

The Hebrew alphabet only contains 22 characters, so numeric values were calculated by combined letters. This combination method was also true of the Greek system of numbers (each letter of the alphabet has a numerical value) and it is true of Roman numerals as well (and we still find Roman numerals in use today).

The ancient Greeks used a system and alphabet similar to the Hebrew alphabet; here are a few letters for comparison.

Hebrew	Greek
Aleph א	Alpha α
Bet ב	Beta β
Daled ד	Delta δ
Lamed ל	Lambda λ

Out of the Hebrew tradition grew the mystical Kabbalah, and its central symbol, the Kabbalist Tree of Life, which represents the emanation of the universe. Numbers were very important to the Kabbalists, and they used the Hebrew alphabet to enumerate each stage of development on the Tree of Life. Each of these numbered emanations is called a Sephira, and they are numbered one (Aleph א) to ten (Yod י). Each number is thought to express the vibration of its Sephira.

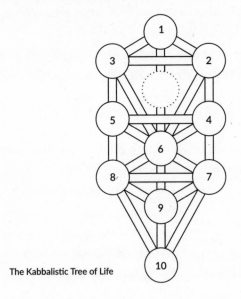

The Kabbalistic Tree of Life

One of the earliest forms of numerology, called *gematria*, derives from the mystical Kabbalah. Gematria is a method of interpreting mystical scripture by computing the numerical value of words (based on the number correspondences of the Hebrew alphabet) and then finding corresponding words with the same value. In gematria, two words are mystically equivalent if they add up to the same number. For example, the Hebrew words for "love" and "one" both have the numerical value of 13; this mystical connection thus reinforces the belief that "the **One** God is **Love**."

The numerology of Kabbalah is a fascinating separate study, but it is not a system widely used by modern numerologists.

The Romans

The Romans also used letters as numbers and we know these today as "Roman numerals." Here are a few examples:

M C IX V III

M	= 1,000
C	= 100
L	= 50
X	= 10
V	= 5
I	= 1
IX	= 10 minus 1 (left), therefore 9
XI	= 10 plus 1 (right), therefore 11
IV	= 5 minus 1, therefore 4
VI	= 5 plus 1, therefore 6

As you can see, these alphabet number systems were cumbersome, and none of them included a zero. The number systems were useful for counting, but true mathematics was not born until the time of Pythagoras.

True Numbers

The number system that we use in the West today is called the Arabic system or Arabic numbers. This system actually came from India, but Persian and Arab traders used it because it was simple to use, it worked for math, and it was universal. It wasn't attached to any particular nation or alphabet, as were the Roman, Greek, and Hebrew systems, so it had no national or religious connotations.

The Basic
Method of
Numerology

2

The numerical system we use today, the Arabic system, is a "base 10" alphabet of numbers. That means we count from 0 to 9, and then begin a second set from 10 to 19, and then 20 to 29, and so forth.

The practice of numerology is based on the Pythagorean system of 1 through 9 (the concept of "zero" was not even postulated until 1,000 years after Pythagoras!) This Pythagorean system is also know as the Western system of numerology. It is the easiest numerology method to learn and the easiest to work with.

Your Basic Tool Kit

Using numbers together with the table of keywords on page 15, you will be able to look at your own personal character and study the temperament of others. You need no special talent or psychic skill, and you do not have to be a mathematician to understand it, because there are no formulas or equations to memorize. Numerology is fun, simple, yet scientific, so it will enable you to pinpoint areas that you can work on for your personal growth.

The Name Number

Old time numerologists used to insist that, when you look into the vibrations of your name, you should use the name that is on your birth certificate. Many modern numerologists consider this an outdated idea, unless you continue to use your birth name throughout your life. People change their names for many reasons—by marriage, through gender transformation, or by whim.

Some people use one name among close friends and another in business (a pet name such as Niki instead of the more formal Nicole), some people use a pen name for their creative work, and some people have permanently adopted a shortened version of their birth name (such as Kate) and never go by its original (Kathleen, or Katherine). The name you use today is who you are at this moment in time, and that is the name you should work with numerologically to determine your name number.

Having said that, however, you might find it interesting to try out the system using your birth name and any other names you have used in the course of your lifetime. You will be able to see whether these name changes have affected your behavior or character at different times of your life or under different circumstances, such as before or after marriage.

The chart below is the numerology table we will be working with. You may wish to copy it down so that it is easy to refer to, until you become familiar with it and have it memorized.

1	2	3	4	5	6	7	8	9
A	B	C	D	E	F	G	H	I
J	K	L	M	N	O	P	Q	R
S	T	U	V	W	X	Y	Z	

Now let's get to work!

In this book, I have used an imaginary person called James Robert Pearson* and we will use that name in our calculation examples.

---

*I've randomly made this name up, and it is not meant to represent any real person living or dead.

Start by finding the numbers that correspond to each letter in your name, and make a note of it. You will end up with a string of numbers like this:

J	a	m	e	s		R	o	b	e	r	t		P	e	a	r	s	o	n
1	1	4	5	1		9	6	2	5	9	2		7	5	1	9	1	6	5

Now shrink the numbers down to a single digit by adding the numbers together. Just study the following examples and you will soon get the idea. The first thing we did above was to find the numbers that correspond to every letter in James' name.

Now add all the numbers together to see what they come to. You can do it in one go, or a piece at a time. You'll come up with the same results.

Here are both methods:

James   Robert   Pearson
1, 1, 4, 5, 1 + 9, 6, 2, 5, 9, 2 + 7, 5, 1, 9, 1, 6, 5 = 79

James: $1 + 1 + 4 + 5 + 1$ = 12
Robert: $9 + 6 + 2 + 5 + 9 + 2$ = 33
Pearson: $7 + 5 + 1 + 9 + 1 + 6 + 5$ = 34
                                  sum = 79

Now we reduce this number by adding $7 + 9$ to make 16.
Then we reduce the number again by adding $1 + 6$ to make 7.

Keep reducing your sums until you come up with a single digit. Easy, right?

Thus, James Robert Pearson's name number is 7.

Using Familiar Name, or Nickname

Let us assume that James Robert Pearson prefers to call himself Jim Pearson and see what happens:

Jim: 1 + 9 + 4   = 5
Pearson: 7 + 5 + 1 + 9 + 1 + 6 + 5 = 34
                    sum   = 39

Now we add 3 + 9 to make 12.

Then 1 + 2 to make 3.

In this method, Jim Pearson's name number is 3.

Keywords for Numerology

The Energy of Numbers and Dynamic Forces

Masculine and feminine numbers (first suggested by Pythagoras) do not have a sexual association. Like ying and yang, they relate to the dynamic forces that govern the energy of number.

Number	Energy	Dynamic Force
1	Personal resources	Masculine
2	Personal feelings	Feminine
3	Personal creativity	Masculine
4	Instinct and logic	Feminine
5	Expansion and sense	Masculine
6	Intuition and theory	Feminine
7	Setting limits	Masculine
8	Transformation	Feminine
9	Spiritual creativity	Masculine

The Color Code

Each number corresponds to a specific color, so once you understand the vibrational energies of the numbers, you can choose to wear certain colors to tap into them.

Number	Number	Vibrational Energy
1	Light green	The Physical Body
2	Dark Green	The Emotions
3	Pink	Creativity
4	Black	The Material World
5	Yellow	Intellect
6	Brown	Effectiveness
7	Blue	Communication
8	Purple	Spirituality
9	White	Higher Spirit

Numbers and Astrology

Number	Energy	Planet	Sign	Keyword
1	Ego	Sun	Leo	Positive
2	Caring	Moon	Cancer	Feelings
3	Action	Mars	Aries	Initiative
4	Instincts	Mercury	Gemini/Virgo	Thought
5	Learning	Jupiter	Sagittarius	Expansion
6	Imagination	Venus	Taurus/Libra	Discrimination
7	Time	Neptune	Pisces	Intuition
8	Transformation	Pluto	Scorpio	Subconscious
9	Karma	Neptune	Pisces	Spirituality
10	Intellectual	Uranus	Aquarius	Originality

The Number Chapters

Now you can move on and discover what the various numbers can tell you about yourself or others in your life. Certain of the following chapters will show you how you and others are operating right now, but other chapters will show the karma that you brought with you into the world when you were born. This will show the benefits and energies with which you were born, and the aspects of your life where you might still have some work to do.

Later chapters show you how to predict events, and offer suggestions about compatibility with other people.

Your
Name
Number

3

Numerological theory suggests that you always use the full name on your birth certificate when working out your name number, but as I mentioned in chapter 1, it is also interesting to see how a change of name can affect your outlook. Many women marry and change their name to their husband's family name (and some retain their birth name), but other changes are a matter of choice, or simply a matter of shortening a name—Mike Smith rather than Michael Edward Smith, for example. So begin by using the name on your birth certificate, and then use the system again with the name you go by on a day-to-day basis.

Here is the alphabet table again. Use the table as shown in the previous chapter and keep reducing your total until you end up with a number between 1 and 9.

1	2	3	4	5	6	7	8	9
A	B	C	D	E	F	G	H	I
J	K	L	M	N	O	P	Q	R
S	T	U	V	W	X	Y	Z	

(Note: If you end up with 11 or 22, make a special note of this. These two numbers are considered "master numbers," and have a special significance in numerology. We will discuss these special numbers in later chapters on karma and destiny. But for now, you can reduce 11 to 2, and 22 to 4).

Number 1

Vibration: The Sun

Associations: Benevolence, creativity and protection

Sun sign: Leo

Symbol: The Lion

Kabbalah: Unity, wholeness, totality

Keywords: Ego, personal identity, leadership, purposeful, tenacious

Days of the month: 1, 10, 19, 28

Number 1 people dislike criticism. They have a strong sense of their own worth, so they usually demand and get respect from others. These folk insist on controlling and organizing everyone and everything and they hold quite definite views, so they can be stubborn when thwarted. There is an underlying desire to be original, creative, and inventive. Anything they undertake can result in a rise to a position of authority and they often insist that everyone look up to them—and this includes friends, family, colleagues, and even the boss. Without the respect of others, they take out their resentment and frustration on anyone who happens to be around.

A Number 1 person will shoulder burdens, protect the weak, and defend the helpless, as long as the hapless person does exactly as he is told. These individuals always think they know better than anyone else does, and they are quite certain that their opinions are flawless. Most of the time, they are right, and this annoys everyone else—especially those who are required to listen to their lectures.

Number 1 people are very susceptible to sincere compliments. When they know that others genuinely appreciate them, they will do anything to please and can be outstandingly kind and generous. Love—both giving and receiving—is as vital as breathing to number 1.

When someone shows them up or wounds their pride, they can become most unpleasant. These individuals will forget slights quite quickly, but only after suitably humble apologies—the only way to end a confrontation with a Number 1 person. They treat those who they trust and love with warmth and affection, but familiarity from strangers causes deep resentment.

Number 1 loves children and young people. Often there is sadness connected with a child. Clothes, jewels, and flashy cars are a basic requirement. These people have an unmistakable sense of inbred dignity. An ideal career is a creative or manual job that allows a measure of authority and freedom from restriction.

Their weak areas include the heart or circulation, eye trouble, or poor vision.

Number Two

Vibration: The Moon

Associations: Dreams, conception, childbirth, parenthood, imagination, sensitivity

Sun sign: Cancer

Symbol: The Crab

Kabbalah: Division, relatedness

Keywords: Feeling, caring, balanced, sensitive, cheerful, team worker

Days of the month: 2, 11, 20, 29

Number 2 people fear the unfamiliar or the unknown. They are not always as forceful as they need to be when carrying out ideas and plans, but they are inventive and imaginative. These people have a romantic nature and their intuition is often highly developed. They may fear every kind of loss imaginable —love, property, friendship, money, work —or the loss of relationships through separation or death. They love to travel, but they need a secure home base. Often devoted to their parents, particularly the mother, they must be careful not to smother their children by being over possessive.

All Number 2 people are concerned with family and friends. They tend to hover and try to ensure that their loved ones do not make unsuitable friendships, catch cold, or throw money away in foolish ventures. They seek partners in love and in business, as they don't always feel that they can cope alone. Ultra cautious, they hate gambling or taking chances. Although they love money, they prefer to save it in secure investments and to increase their capital with interest and dividends.

These most secretive individuals never confide in anyone. They manage to wheedle out other people's secrets but they protect their own privacy. They will often appear to be undecided, and then they will make an unexpected move, sometimes with a surprising degree of aggression. Their careers might include teaching, caring for children, or writing stories for children.

Their weak areas are the lungs, breasts, chest, and stomach.

Number 3

Vibration: Mars

Associations: Service and direct action

Sun sign: Aries

Symbol: The Ram

Kabbalah: Fertility, completion

Keywords: Creative, versatile, adaptable, idealistic, charming

Days of the month: 3, 12, 21, 30

Number 3 people want nothing less than the truth; they cannot be fooled by deception and they can spot a phony a mile off. Do not attempt to bother them with lies, dishonesty, or even a mild distortion of the truth. Some Number 3 individuals actually manage to achieve their ultimate goal of truthfulness while others mislead themselves into believing their own illusions, and for them the search for reality never ends.

Fiercely independent, these subjects will not allow others to tie them down, and they will always demand total freedom of speech and movement. Travel is a necessity for them and they need opportunities to see the world, to learn about foreign countries, and to mix with a wide variety of people. Number 3 people are passionately interested in philosophy and intellectual concepts. They have their own contagious brand of optimism and they look on the bright side of everything. These individuals can spend their lives in a quest for truth, and they can be religious, fiercely agnostic, or atheist. Because the concept of religion or philosophy is a vital part of their life, it is never a neutral issue and is either accepted or rejected with fervor or fanaticism.

Expect these individuals to speak bluntly and to offer direct and candid opinions. These people show fierce loyalty to their pets and to all animals and they will always defend the underdog (animal or human) in any dispute. Total freedom within the bounds of marriage and family is the only way for them.

Number 3 subjects are attracted to gambling, tests of physical strength, and risk taking in all its forms, and they enjoy playing or watching rough sports. They prefer jobs that allow them to get around, they enjoy being in positions of authority, and they can enjoy working in military or government occupations.

A Number 3 personality is a strange blend of the happy-go-lucky clown and the wise philosopher. They can be so two-sided that one day they will be perfectly sensible, and the next day almost completely crazy. Their ambitions, dreams, and goals may sometimes be serious and attainable, but often they are just frivolous. More heart than head, their emotions are in control of their minds, so their attitudes and decisions will depend upon whether they are in the mood to be sensible, jolly, silly, or whether they have worked themselves into such a rage that they are capable of saying or doing just about anything.

Their weak areas are the lower spine, leading to sciatica, and skin complaints. They can suffer from anxiety and nervous problems through overwork.

Number 4

Vibration: Mercury

Associations: Instincts, logic, the material world, and the intellect

Sun sign: Gemini/Virgo

Kabbalah: Solidity, reliability, the law

Symbol: The Twins/the Virgin

Keywords: Hard working, sensible, logical, materialistic

Days of the month: 4, 13, 22, 31

Frequently, the family and friends of Number 4 people misunderstand them. Number 4s make their own enigmatic rules that do not always correspond to those of society. Every thought and action is marked with a peculiar individuality. Their speech and actions often shock others and this sometimes seems to be deliberate. If there is an unconventional way of going about something, the Number 4 person will find it. These people care little for the present because their concerns are for the future, so they are frequently light-years ahead of the rest of us. They seem to have an inborn talent for prophecy and for knowing what will happen or what will be fashionable long before it arrives.

The lifestyle of Number 4 people is usually unconventional, but their crazy ideas often turn out to be surprisingly successful. The curious nature of these individuals draws them to anything that is off the beaten track. Any incredible, unscientific, or unproven theory excites the Number 4 person and this individual can be convinced (and convince everyone else) that a peculiar notion can be turned into reality. Never tell this subject that something is impossible; this simply spurs Number 4 on to prove you wrong.

In every area of life, the vibration of Number 4 is one of change, but these unusual people are often reluctant to change their own personal habits, as they can be both fixed and stubborn. When others ask them to become more socially acceptable, they resist.

While money has little or no meaning, friendships are vital. Number 4 people have no desire to impress others and they don't even care where they live, as long as they can keep their imaginations intact. These people genuinely fail to notice their surroundings. They believe in "live and let live"; but in return, they expect to be given the same consideration by others. They enjoy working in the fields of building, architecture, and design.

Their weak spots are the kidneys and bladder, plus headaches and nervous tension.

Number 5

Vibration: Jupiter

Associations: Expansion, tolerance, communication, versatility and movement

Sun sign: Sagittarius

Symbol: The Archer

Kabbalah: Life, regeneration, creativity, expansion

Keywords: Education, travel, philosophy, liveliness, creativity, artistry

Days of the month: 5, 14, 23

Number 5 people are innately courteous and charming, but if they spot flaws and mistakes, they will not hesitate to point them out. These people cannot ignore their own mistakes or those of others, so they frequently beat themselves up and lay blame on others. Change is a necessity to them in all areas of their lives and they adore travel and movement. Because it is hard for them to rely on their intuition and feelings, they may over-analyze situations and people. This can cause breakdowns in their relationships because no partnership can bear the pressure of constant scrutiny. Number 5s can talk a love affair to death. They do not understand that love has nothing to do with logic.

They make pleasant company, because outwardly they are fun and cooperative. Number 5 is the vibration of the higher intellect. These are extremely bright people, always mentally alert, and with higher than average intelligence. As they are fine-tuned to notice the tiniest detail, they never miss a trick. They know instinctively how to use the space that they inhabit, and if money pressures prevent them from traveling, they will daydream and travel in their minds. Their vivid imaginations are enough to satisfy their wandering urges.

Traditionally, the Number 5 is associated with earth magic. These people often long to believe in magic, fairies, and anything mysterious. However, their need to analyze every detail is at odds with this, so they frequently find it hard to understand themselves.

Number 5 people are unusually highly strung. They crave excitement and live on their nerves. Their ability to think and act quickly means that they often act impulsively. At heart, they are speculators with a keen sense for new inventions and a willingness to take risks. Successful occupations are likely to be writing, publishing, advertising, public relations, sales, teaching, speculation, and the travel trade. Those ruled by Number 5 are blessed with a flexible point of view. They have the ability to recover from bad experiences and move on.

Health problems might include insomnia, neuritis, and nervous problems.

Number 6

Vibration: Venus

Associations: Abstract thinking, fantasy, creativity and imagination

Sun sign: Taurus/Libra

Symbol: The Bull/The Scales

Kabbalah: Fruitfulness, harmony, the home

Keywords: Imagination, theory, balance, harmony

Days of the month: 6, 15, 24

These people have a magnetism that is attractive, and their families, friends, and associates genuinely love them. They are devoted to their loved ones and they know how to show it. Idealism rather than sex motivates the nature of Number 6 people and they are born romantics, with a streak of sentimentality that is impossible for them to deny or hide. They love harmony in their surroundings and they adore music and art. They try to live in beautiful homes with the most tasteful furnishings.

Making others happy and entertaining friends come high on their personal list of important activities. They do not like confrontation, and cannot face jealousy, discord, arguments, or unpleasantness of any sort. Number 6 people make friends easily and they enjoy being the diplomat in negotiating the disputes of their relatives and friends. They appear to be the most docile and amenable people until they are crossed; then their stubborn nature kicks in.

Money often comes without effort, sometimes through inheritance and sometimes through the way that they use their abilities and talents. They often can veer between extravagance and stinginess. They may work in the arts, the media, entertainment, or some aspect of the health and fitness industry, especially anything that is associated with dieting.

Most Number 6 people love the countryside and they find it emotionally soothing to live or spend time near trees or water. They find anything ugly very offensive and they are very fond of luxury in all its forms. They hate vulgarity or loud behavior and will always show the highest admiration for anything that is tasteful and refined. These subjects invariably have impeccable manners and are always polite, but they do not hesitate to make their opinions clear whenever they have strong feelings about something. Discussion and debate come easily to them. Their logical minds usually win others over to their point of view. They have an irresistible smile.

Weak spots are the throat, larynx, nose, and lungs. They can suffer from circulatory problems, and are prone to weight gain due to insufficient exercise.

Number 7

Vibration: Neptune

Associations: The bridge to the spiritual world

Sun sign: Pisces

Symbol: The Two Fishes

Kabbalah: Mysticism, magic, spirituality

Keywords: Spiritual, sensitive, intuitive

Days of the month: 7, 16, 25

Number 7 people often have amazing dreams. Sometimes they tell others about them and sometimes they just keep quiet about them. They have a secret interest in unknown mysteries, UFOs, and mythology—in fact, they are attracted to anything that is esoteric and occult. These people are often intuitive and clairvoyant, with magnetic and calming personalities. These individuals have strange and unorthodox ideas about religion, politics, or just life in general. Following the herd is not for them, although they can be attracted to the latest religious cult.

A Number 7 person will probably become a seasoned traveler who enjoys reading travel books and soaking up information about foreign countries and people. There may be a strong attraction to the sea, so they may take up water sports, sailing, or spend their lives at work on the sea.

These individuals prefer to work in the arts or the entertainment industry, and while they can make good money at times, they are aware that their success is likely to be short lived. They don't bother much with material possessions or money in the normal run of things. They may make significant contributions to charities, but in a quiet way.

It is unlikely to hear a Number 7 person talk much about their ambitions, because the things that they involve themselves in have a philosophical tinge. Fortunate friends and family of Number 7 folk know that their loved one will stand up for them and offer a sympathetic and understanding ear when needed.

Number 7s have a sensitive nature, an artistic temperament, and the most refined manners. These people are truly unprejudiced and non-judgmental. Never expect to get a Number 7 person to tell you what he or she is really thinking; these individuals live in a world of secret dreams and only divulge these to those whom they trust most.

This number is the symbol of the ancient Greek god, Chronos, who reminds us that things that have a limited duration are not real. Number 7 is symbolic of totality in the material world: 7 notes in the musical scale, 7 colors of the rainbow, 7 virtues, 7 deadly sins, 7 chakras in the body, 7 planets known to the ancient world, and 7 days of the week.

Skin complaints may be a problem, but bad diet and worry can also make them ill.

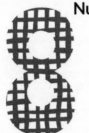

Number 8

Vibration: Pluto

Associations: Practical matters, the unconscious, transformation

Sun sign: Scorpio

Symbol: The Phoenix/Scorpion/Eagle

Kabbalah: Material concerns, leadership, justice, ambition

Keywords: Ambitious, self sufficient, persistent

Days of the month: 8, 17, 26

These people are reserved and quiet. They are not pushy, but they usually get where they want to go, slowly and surely, to achieve their ambitions. Their shy manner is a cover for an intense drive to get to the top. The areas in which the Number 8 operates are money, sex, and power. These individuals are patient people who are quite happy to wait for their plans to bear fruit. It is unusual to find them procrastinating. Their sense of responsibility and duty does not allow them to waste time and they can be relied on to do what others expect of them. They find careers in public life, large organizations, and jobs that offer challenge and excitement, such as fund raising and big business.

Their sense of humor is subtle and dry, which makes them amusing company. They may behave as though they don't care what others think of them, but secretly, they enjoy compliments and sincere appreciation and they hate to be thought stupid or wrong.

There is an enormous inner strength in most Number 8 people, and they harbor deep, intense natures. They often find that they have an important role to play in the lives of others and some-times they can be fanatical about religion. Although they make many loving friends, they also make bitter enemies. They may seem to be undemonstrative and cold toward those whom they love and trust. Although they show affection shyly, in reality they are devoted to their friends and family. Underneath a cool surface lurks loneliness and a desperate need to be loved. When it is necessary, they may go to great lengths to make sacrifices for a strongly held ambition or ideal, or for those who depend on them.

With age and maturity, Number 8 people look and behave younger than their years. They demand much of themselves and others, but for all their appearance of discipline, maturity and self-control, deep down they are needy and lonely. The wholehearted pursuit of happiness is difficult for them.

Their health issues might include liver problems, rheumatism, headaches, and diseases of the blood.

Number 9

Vibration: Neptune

Associations: Divine love, completion, talent, spirituality and karma

Sun sign: Pisces

Symbol: The Fishes

Kabbalah: Humanitarian issues, inspirational leadership

Keywords: Creative, spiritual, compassionate

Days of the month: 9, 18, 27

These folk are determined to get their own way. They can be impulsive and prone to make snap decisions, and then live to regret their hasty actions. Although Number 9 people have a temper, they soon forgive and forget.

Their trusting nature means that others can lead them into trouble. They are direct and straightforward, they expect others to be the same, and they are disappointed when they discover that others can be manipulative or devious—because they are incapable of such behavior themselves. They need to be more cautious and less trusting. These subjects can be relied upon to show understanding, compassion, and the highest ideals of selfless love. They possess an amazing ability to go straight to the heart of a situation, bypassing the need for lengthy analysis. Slower thinkers get on their nerves. At times, their impatience with others does not win them friends or allies.

These subjects have a touchingly childlike quality of vulnerability that drives others to protect them. Some people may think Number 9s are foolish and unworthy of respect, but once others experience the courageous spirit (and violent temper) of the Number 9, they think again. Although these people often appear to be vain, this vanity and concern about their own appearance derives from lack of confidence and fear of rejection. They may appear to be assertive, independent, and pushy, but in reality they need constant reassurance that others love, like, admire, and respect them.

Often very extravagant and very generous to others, they will instinctively let tomorrow take care of itself; they let go of everything and just *give*. These individuals always tune in to happiness and joy. They choose to work in the spheres of art, writing, music, religious work, theater, and entertainment. Surprisingly, some opt for a career in the military. These folk are excellent advisers.

Health problems relate to fever and they have delicate stomachs, possibly owing to nerves and tension.

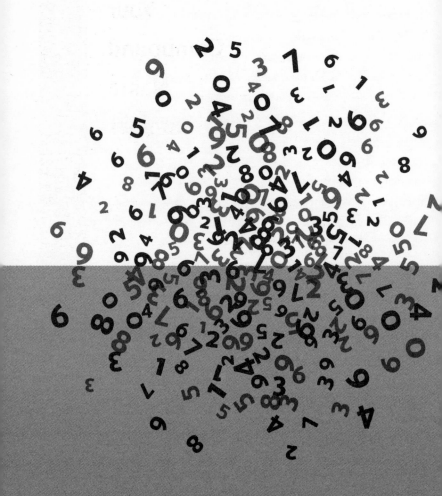

Your
Compound
Name
Number

4

A compound name number is similar to your name number, but in this case you are reducing your number to two digits—thus the term "compound." You can use your popular name or nickname, or use the name on your birth certificate. There is one caveat: your final name number must be 30 or below. If this process of reduction bypasses the range between 10 and 30, then this chapter does not apply to you.

Why bother to compute a compound name number? This system is though to have its origins in Chaldean times, 300 to 200 years *before* Pythagoras. This is an ancient system. The single digit number is thought to merely represent the external or visible nature of a person's name. The compound, two-digit number, on the other hand, is thought to represent the hidden or metaphysical forces and vibrations of a person's name. The compound name number may even show hidden influences, or predict the future.

Using the compound name number method will give you an additional layer of insight into the vibrations of your name.

We will again use our imaginary individual from chapter one as an example.

In the case of James Robert Pearson, when we added his numbers together, the result came to 79. This number is above 30, so we continue to reduce it by adding the 7 and 9 to make 16. This is now a two-digit number that is below 30.

James: $1 + 1 + 4 + 5 + 1$ = 12
Robert: $9 + 6 + 2 + 5 + 9 + 2$ = 33
Pearson: $7 + 5 + 1 + 9 + 1 + 6 + 5$ = 34
                                    = <u>79</u>

Now we add $7 + 9$ to get 16.

However, let's say you have a name number that initially adds up to 24. No reduction of that number is necessary. Your compound number name is under 30.

Here are a list of keywords for each compound name number.

10: The Wheel of Fortune

- Ten is the number of rise and fall, it represents good or evil, depending upon the action the person chooses to take.
- It is the number of extreme responses, such as fear, hate, or obsession.
- This number allows a person to understand his power and to use it wisely.
- It represents the power to take a creative concept and turn it into something concrete.
- The subject must be self-disciplined and compassionate.
- This individual must avoid arrogance or lashing out when frustrated.

11: The Clenched Fist

- This number represents treachery and problems that seem to come from nowhere.
- 11 represents two opposing situations or individuals who may eventually separate, which causes difficulties.
- The person needs to learn to compromise and to avoid those things that cause splits in partnerships and relationships.

- Two separate desires or forces may unite and bring happiness, or they may bring conflict and cause separation.

12: The Victim

- This number represents the victim who chooses or is forced to make sacrifices so that others can achieve their ends.
- The subject must be alert in every situation and must watch out for false flattery or hidden agendas.
- This person must guard against being used by others for their own gain.
- If this person is offered a position of authority, that opportunity should be questioned, as it may not be all that it appears to be on its face.
- In order to achieve intellectual and spiritual wisdom, Number 12 will need to make sacrifices and look for solutions from within.
- If the individual takes the trouble to learn and to gain an education, he will overcome suffering and achieve eventual success, so the number represents education, teachers, and students.

13: Transformation

- 13 is NOT an unlucky number.
- This person can achieve a position of power and authority.
- This symbolizes breaking new ground, new discoveries, and explorers.

- The power associated with Number 13 can bring personal destruction if it is used selfishly.
- This number warns of the unexpected and unknown.
- Use the strength of this vibration to adapt to new circumstances.

14: Challenge

- This number represents the media, publishing, and writing.
- Partnerships and businesses will be of great benefit, but the subject must avoid trusting others too much.
- Luck comes with speculation; both gains and losses are likely to be temporary.
- This is a fortunate number for travel with others.
- This is the number of the inner voice, intuition, and self-reliance; however, the individual must guard against overconfidence.

15: The Magician

- This person can make others happy and he can shine light into the darkness.
- The individual has a dramatic temperament, personal magnetism, charisma, and eloquence.
- This is fortunate for obtaining money, favors, and gifts.
- Whenever it is associated with the numbers 4 and 8, this number can be associated with black magic, or with becoming a victim of magic

16: The Shattered Citadel

- This number warns of accidents and it advises the subject to make careful plans before undertaking anything important.
- The person must pay careful attention to detail and anticipate problems.
- Dreams and the person's inner voice may warn of danger in good times.
- Success and happiness come in strange ways, but not via leadership, fame, or celebrity.

17: The Star

- The eight-sided star of Venus is associated with this number, and it represents love and peace.
- Number 17 is associated with the ancient magi.
- This number promises a spiritual rise above trials and tribulations as well as the ability to overcome former failures in career and personal relationships.
- This is a fortunate compound number, representing immortality.

18: Conflict

- Number 18 symbolizes bitter quarrels and family disputes.
- This warns that going after too many material things can retard one's spiritual growth.

- This is the number of social revolution, wars, and upheaval.
- This number brings warnings of treachery and deception from both enemies and friends.
- Money or status may come as a result of conflict.
- The subject must beware of danger from natural disasters or electric shocks.
- The individual must meet hatred and deception with generosity, forgiveness, love, and kindness because love will always conquer conflict.

19: The Sun

- This is one of the most fortunate of the compound numbers, as it indicates victory over disappointment and failure.
- Any negative vibrations will be diluted by this number, which blesses the individual and promises fulfillment, happiness, and personal success.
- All ventures should go smoothly.

20: Judgment

- This symbolizes a powerful awakening, which will bring new purpose, plans, and ambition.
- This brings a clear call to action.
- Faith in the personal power to transform will conquer delays.

- This is not the number of financial success, as it applies to personal happiness and achievement.

21: The Universe

- This number brings advancement, honors, and success.
- After a long struggle, there will be victory.
- This number represents the final victory over all opposition plus karmic rewards.

22: Caution

- This warns against living in a fool's paradise.
- It represents a dreamer who only wakes up when surrounded by danger.
- This is a clear warning of putting too much faith in others.
- The individual should avoid those who are untrustworthy, and always exercise caution.
- The subject must understand that the power to make life changes and prevent failure lies in his own hands, so he must focus on success.

23: The Lion

- This number brings success in the career and personal life.
- People in authority offer help and protection.
- This number offers strength, the ability to face challenges and to win.

24: Creativity

- The person can expect help from people in authority and positions of power.
- This number brings success, especially in the arts, the law, and in love.
- The subject has a magnetic personality and can attract lovers.
- Self-indulgence and arrogance can cause disappointments in career, finance, and personal relationships.
- The subject must never allow good fortune make him careless about spiritual values.
- He must resist the temptation to overindulge or to become selfish.

25: Analysis

- Learning from experience will bring worldly success
- Disappointments that the subject overcomes in early life will help to make him strong.
- This person has excellent powers of judgment.

26: Partnerships

- 26 represents helping others, compassion, and an unselfish attitude.
- The subject will suffer disappointment and failure, which are usually brought about by following bad advice.

27: The Scepter

- The subject will rise to a position of authority.
- This is a fortunate compound number, touched with enchantment, harmony, and courage.
- There are likely to be substantial rewards when the person uses imagination and intellect.
- This person should never allow himself to be intimidated or influenced by the opinions of others.
- It is important for 27 to bring bright ideas and plans to a conclusion.

28: The Lamb

- This person can achieve success, but must guard against later losses, especially from lawsuits.
- Loss comes about through misplaced trust in others and opposition from enemies or competitors in business.
- This individual may have to pull himself up by the bootstraps and start again.
- The phrase "Look before you leap" is the key to this number.

29: Grace Under Pressure

- This person must accept responsibility and not blame others when things go wrong.
- A series of trials and tribulations will test this individual's spiritual strength.

- The subject must avoid unreliable friends who can deceive him or make him feel uncertain about his own judgment.
- The opposite sex may be the cause of anxiety and grief.
- The individual must develop an optimistic outlook and learn to believe in himself.

30: Meditation

- Success depends upon the individual, as this person has few real friends.
- The subject will learn by going on an inward journey and considering spiritual rather than material matters.
- This individual may be a loner by nature or this may be a temporary situation.
- This person can turn ideas into something worthwhile, and while he may be alone much of the time, it appears that he prefers it that way.

Your
Personality
Number

5

The personality number represents the face you show to the world. When calculating this number, it is best to use the name you usually call yourself, rather than your full birth name.

Count the consonants in your name and ignore the vowels. (You may consider Y as a vowel for this method.) Reduce the result to a single digit or 11 and 22 for this chapter.

1	2	3	4	5	6	7	8	9
A	B	C	D	E	F	G	H	I
J	K	L	M	N	O	P	Q	R
S	T	U	V	W	X	Y	Z	

In the case of our imaginary person, Jim Pearson, he would only add together the numbers that represent the letters, J, M, P, R, S and N as follows:

J = 1, M = 4, P = 7, R = 9, S = 1, N = 5

Therefore:

$1 + 4 + 7 + 9 + 1 + 5 = 27$

$2 + 7 = 9$

Jim Pearson's personality number is 9.

Here are keywords for the traits of personality numbers.

Number 1

- An appearance of confidence usually masks feelings of uncertainty.
- A natural leader who assumes responsibility.
- Many good friends.
- May be arrogant and pushy.
- Over-demanding behavior can alienate friends and colleagues.

Number 2

- Striving for perfection.
- The search for harmony and balance can attract criticism.
- Hard for others to live with.
- The subject must learn to trust and allow others to be wrong sometimes.

Number 3

- Loneliness lies behind a cheerful, sociable, popular, confident appearance.
- Sometimes dresses very extravagantly.
- This natural actor adores the center stage and has masses of energy.
- Can be boastful and conceited, but this subject is a real softie underneath.

Number 4

- A trustworthy, loyal, dependable partner.
- Hates innovation, change, and anything unconventional.
- The subject should chill out, be less conservative.
- Must allow others to have their opinions.

Number 5

- Well-read, inquisitive, or a restless gossip.
- Great companion, excellent friend.
- This person may travel a great deal for fun or business purposes.
- Many changes of address and connections with other countries.

Number 6

- Has an easy-going attitude to life.
- Hates disagreements and problems.
- Places great value on beauty and luxury.
- Charming, but sometimes selfish.

Number 7

- Reserved and difficult to get to know, standoffish.
- Underneath a cool exterior is an interesting, friendly personality.

- Often a wealth of information on anything related to mysticism.
- May be psychic.

Number 8

- Demanding, bossy, but hard on himself as well as on others.
- A good employer with a shrewd understanding of finances.
- An excellent organizer who will always rise to a challenge.
- Loves the best of everything for himself and his family.

Number 9

- Fun, energetic, exuding charm, sex appeal, and magnetism.
- This person hates restriction, so he has many relationships.
- This individual is a terrible time keeper.
- Interested in spiritual matters.

Number 11

- This person makes enemies unintentionally.
- Cannot stand those who disagree with him.
- Given time, this person becomes a faithful, loyal friend.
- Needs a secure emotional life.

Number 22

- Always ready with help and advice.
- Maintains inner strength and wisdom and has sound judgment.
- Happy, attractive person who makes a wonderful friend.
- A wonderful builder, designer, or architect.

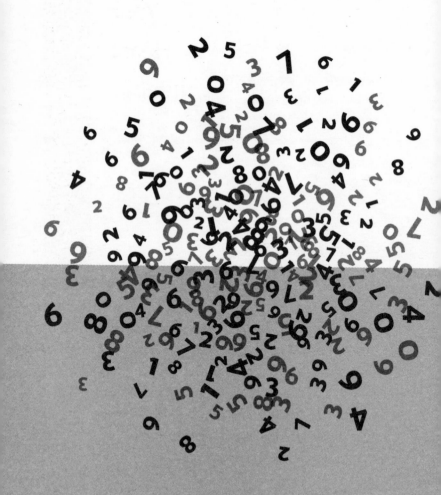

Your Heart Number

6

The heart number reveals your personal feelings and deepest wishes. Most of us keep these hidden—sometimes even from ourselves—so this number will help you to understand what motivates your instinctive behavior. It will also help you see your hidden talents. The heart number makes it easier to understand your true needs when making important decisions. It also gives you an idea of what motivates others.

It is best to use the name that you usually call yourself for this. If a heart number comes to 11 or 22, leave this as is rather than reducing the number any further.

To calculate the heart number, use only the vowels of a name.

1	2	3	4	5	6	7	8	9
A	B	C	D	E	F	G	H	I
J	K	L	M	N	O	P	Q	R
S	T	U	V	W	X	Y	Z	

Therefore, in the case of our friend, Jim Pearson, he would only add up I, E, A and O.

I = 9, E = 5, A = 1, O   = 6
9 + 5 + 1 + 6   = 21
2 + 1   = 3

Jim Pearson's heart number is 3.

Here are the keywords for your heart number.

Number 1

- Born leader who is confident and purposeful.
- High energy level, determination and ambition creates success.
- Does not give enough time or energy to the love life.

Number 2

- Sensitive, kind, vulnerable, and needing emotional security.
- An overwhelming desire to give to and care for others.
- Gifted healer or therapist.

Number 3

- Eternal optimist with a sense of humor.
- A tough exterior hides a fear of rejection or abandonment.
- Great parent, reliable partner, and wonderful friend.

Number 4

- Shy and sensitive, so shuns the limelight, preferring family life.
- Born homemaker who needs comfortable, spotless surroundings.
- May build or improve a home.

Number 5

- Relationships can bring problems, but friendships succeed.
- Dislikes authority and restriction.
- May study alone or find others to share their views.

Number 6

- Love is the key to happiness, but it may take time to arrive.
- Puts the needs of others first.
- Needs praise and support to feel totally confident and relaxed.

Number 7

- This individual is happy to be alone.
- Could be a mystic or philosopher.
- Close relationships make this person uncomfortable.

Number 8

- Feels secure when in control.
- Good organizer, but moody when things don't go his way.
- Often unable to relax and let go.

Number 9

- Good organizer who loves variety, challenge, and changes of scene.
- Problem solver, a good mechanic who likes to know how things work.
- Can have a clinical attitude to relationships.

Number 11

- Makes a decision and sticks to it stubbornly.
- Despite being self-reliant, this person needs to feel wanted.
- Ideals and principles are important.

Number 22

- If this person gets a grip on reality, he can achieve whatever he wants.
- Charming companion and great friend.
- Can create an atmosphere of peace and harmony.

Your
Life Path
Number

7

The life path number provides a general overview of the personal traits that will assist you on your life's path—the path of opportunities and hardships you will encounter. The life path number will reveal your strengths and weaknesses on that path.

To calculate the life path number, you will be using an individual's date of birth. You can reduce this to two digits, as long as the numbers fall between 1 and 21. If we look at the following two examples, you will see how to do this.

Date of birth: January 2, 1970 (month 1, day 2, year 1970)
Addition: $1 + 2 + 1 + 9 + 7 + 0 = 20$

Number 20 comes between 12 and 21, *so it is within the range.*

Date of birth: May 2, 1982 (month 5, day 2, year 1982)
Addition: $5 + 2 + 1 + 9 + 8 + 2 = 27$

Number 27 *is outside the range*, so we reduce it by adding the 2 and the 7 to make 9.

Number 1

- A purposeful leader.
- Creative if there is sufficient opportunity.
- Likes to exercise authority.

Number 2

- Well-balanced and cheerful.
- Sensitive to the needs of others.
- Interested in partnerships, teamwork and politics.

Number 3

- Versatile, adaptable, and easily bored by routine.
- Needs freedom to travel and explore.
- Intuition and common sense lead to success.

Number 4

- Hard-working, sensible, logical, and methodical.
- Can be materialistic and fussy.
- Either very traditional or a real reformer.

Number 5

- Lively, creative and artistic.
- An excellent communicator who may teach or write.
- Loves travel, but balances this with home and family life.

Number 6

- Harmony in the home and among friends is vital.
- A very hard worker who sacrifices himself for others.
- Can succeed in entertainment, writing, the arts or the health industry.

Number 7

- Spiritual, sensitive, intuitive.
- Into alternative therapies, psychism, mysticism.
- Caring, but also attracted to film, poetry, and story-writing.

Number 8

- Ambitious, self-sufficient, persistent.
- A powerful leader or business tycoon.
- Interested in justice and honesty.

Number 9

- Creative, spiritual, compassionate.
- Interested in the theatre and the arts.
- Can be religious, possibly too much so.

Number 10

- Ten represents self-motivation.

- This person is not easily influenced.
- The head of a family and king of his realm at work.

Number 11

- A determined personality who can get things done.
- High principles, but selfishness may spoil good intentions.
- Able to take risks successfully, as long as he is not too self-indulgent.

Number 12

- A number representing emotion and sacrifice.
- Associated with the unseen and secrecy.
- It is essential for this person to grasp educational opportunities.

Number 13

- Linked to positive power when used wisely.
- Represents change and rebirth, upheaval and trauma.
- It is essential for this person to be adaptable.

Number 14

- Challenge and movement.
- Fortunate for money.
- The subject must be cautious when taking risks.

Number 15

- Associated with magic and power.
- Luck and good fortune.
- The subject's life will be dramatic.

Number 16

- Events may not go according to plan.
- A passionate, volatile number.
- This person may be an explorer, inventor or just impulsive and rash.

Number 17

- A spiritual number connected with intuition.
- Sometimes called the number of immortality.
- The subject's life may be difficult.

Number 18

- Linked with the home and family.
- Sometimes a difficult life path.
- The individual must balance material and spiritual matters.

Number 19

- Success, good humor, and happiness.
- Good for speculation and recognition.
- This person will have many dealings with children.

Number 20

- Fate and karma rule here.
- Life will never be boring or dull.
- The person will succeed with plans and new projects.

Number 21

- Denotes power, success, and achievement.
- Success and karmic benefits.
- If the subject is persistent, he will succeed.

Your
Destiny
Number

8

The destiny number shows your destiny and life purpose based on your personality and potential. Find this number by adding together the letters in your full name as it appears on your birth certificate, including any middle names. Keep on reducing the numbers until you end up with a number between 1 and 9, or 11 or 22, then look up the interpretations.

Here is a repeat of the system and the example that appeared in chapter two.

1	2	3	4	5	6	7	8	9
A	B	C	D	E	F	G	H	I
J	K	L	M	N	O	P	Q	R
S	T	U	V	W	X	Y	Z	

I'll use our imaginary subject, James Robert Pearson, as an example.

James: $1 + 1 + 4 + 5 + 1$ $= 12$
Robert: $9 + 6 + 2 + 5 + 9 + 2$ $= 33$
Pearson: $7 + 5 + 1 + 9 + 1 + 6 + 5$ $= \underline{34}$
sum $= \underline{79}$

Now we reduce this number by adding $7 + 9$ to make 16.
Then we reduce the number again by adding $1 + 6$ to make 7.
Thus, James Robert Pearson's destiny number is 7.

Here are descriptions of the destiny number traits.

Number 1

People with this number like to be in charge of events and they can be bossy and dictatorial. Number 1s are the leaders who despise being told what to do, or being retrained or restricted. They like having things their own way. They need to be the center of attention at all times.

These individuals are highly creative and they love to be at the head of a large family. They can be demanding in relationships and their passionate, sexy nature frequently leads them to look for affairs outside marriage or partnership.

Number 2

These people are well balanced, diplomatic, and level-headed, and they create an atmosphere of calm in situations that others find hard to control. They are tactful negotiators, they are protective of others, and they keep their own counsel, so they do well in any job that requires these special talents.

They are loving and protective towards their families, although some of their loved ones find them patronizing and overly-considerate, which makes them feel stifled by the overwhelming attention. A relationship with the right partner can be passionate and successful. These people prefer to be in a partnership in their personal lives and in business.

Number 3

These people are determined to succeed in everything they decide to do and they are bright, cheerful, and enthusiastic. When unhappy or disappointed, they hide their feelings behind

quick wit and humor, so they make excellent actors— and they love an audience. In a similar way, these individuals also make great sales people.

These people often feel lonely and they may not get things right in the area of personal relationships; part of this is because they need freedom while also needing desperately to feel loved and cherished. They are flirtatious and attractive, but despite their talent for attracting interest, this doesn't satisfy them, because what they really need is someone who will be happy to share their life in a loving relationship. Their best attribute is a great sense of humor.

Number 4

These organized people spend their lives making lists. They are methodical, efficient, and systematic, and they make wonderful employees. Many of them remain single throughout their lives, frequently preferring the company of animals to close human relationships. However, they enjoy being involved in local or community matters.

If they marry, it will be to improve their financial or social position. While they can be relied upon to be faithful, they can be difficult to live with, because they cannot compromise and they feel that they have to control every situation and everyone around them.

Number 5

These subjects are hard workers and excellent communicators, who need change and variety to function well. They can become restless if required to concentrate on something they don't want to do, and if this happens, they will find a way of escaping their restrictions. Travel is vital to them and they move around a great deal.

Where relationships are concerned, they love the thrill of the chase and they are flirtatious. In some cases, they take their time about finding a partner or they find it hard to settle down with one partner. They have a strong sex drive, so when the novelty wears off with one partner, they may move on quickly to the next romantic challenge.

Number 6

These people can be very successful being self-employed or owning their own business because they push themselves, work hard, and have very high standards. They can be perfectionists who channel a great deal of energy into doing things properly and also into making money.

They love to make others happy and content, but their attitude to relationships is not always traditional.

They are attractive and loving, but sometimes they are so busy working at their job or keeping up impossible domestic standards that they don't notice when their partner needs love and affection. Loving and faithful, they demand that their partner always looks good. This is partly because these people are into appearances, particularly fashion and clothes, to the point that they may be interested in following a career in the fashion world. They are happy to give their partners money for clothes, cosmetics and beauty, and if money is tight, they will learn to design and make clothes for themselves and their loved ones.

Number 7

These dreamy, philosophical folk want to save the planet, adopt a cause, or embrace mysticism. They excel when they work in a group and especially in a teaching or helping role. Music and the

arts are important to them, and listening to music eases their tensions, and by singing along the can express their romantic feelings.

Although very loving, they cannot stand a clingy partner; they must be free to follow their particular star. These individuals are renowned for their mood swings, and this makes them hard to live with. These attractive, physical, sexy people find it hard to relax into a relationship, so their partners are often left wondering how the Number 7 really feels about them, or what they really want.

Number 8

This is the number of the hardworking business tycoon who thrives on responsibility and makes a success of himself. He expects much of himself, and he has absolutely no time or tolerance for the failings of others.

These individuals are highly organized at work, but they don't leave enough time to focus on their relationships, which may suffer and then wither away. Weaker people are drawn to their apparent strength and energy, but then feel short-changed when the Number 8 suddenly becomes cold and uninterested in them. Frankly, these individuals are often too ambitious to put enough effort into long-term partnerships or marriage, so sooner or later, their partners will drift away and look for love and affection elsewhere. If a Number 8 can find a partner who shares their passion for work or who is happy to work in the same business, they can be passionate, happy, and contented—and then make their partner happy as well. They do make an effort to give time to their children, and most are good to their parents as well, as long as the parents are not demanding or clingy.

Number 9

These highly organized people have such a finely tuned level of intuition that they can make excellent split-second decisions that may appear rash to others. They are impatient and they want everything *now*!

They will not wait for anyone or anything. They enjoy variety and challenges in life and in their work.

In partnerships, they are exceptionally loyal and can be a tower of strength in any crisis, but it can be hard for them to form one-on-one relationships, as they feel more comfortable as part of a group. They make warm, caring, and generous friends and lovers.

Number 11

Communication is important to these people, so they often find employment in the media and in films. They are excellent writers

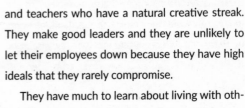

and teachers who have a natural creative streak. They make good leaders and they are unlikely to let their employees down because they have high ideals that they rarely compromise.

They have much to learn about living with others, because they love power and being in control. If they concentrate on a partnership, they will be successful, but it is hard for them to avoid putting their careers first. They have a knack for making influential friends, and this helps them in many different spheres of life.

Number 22

Personal magnetism makes these individuals stand out in a crowd and attract attention, and they often use this to get ahead in their career or job. Idealistic as well as prac-tical, these people are usually successful and they do especially well in design work that combines special sensitivity with an artistic eye. Obvious outlets for their talents are architecture and engineering, or perhaps designing computer software or games.

They are remarkably successful in relationships and they have many admirers. They prefer to be faithful to one partner, although this may not always be reciprocated.

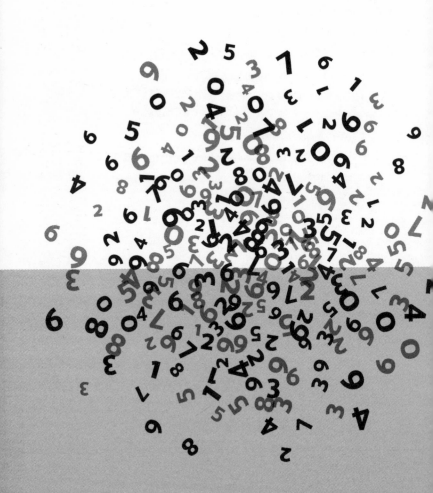

Your
Karmic
Number

9

Your karmic number shows where your faults lie and where you can work on yourself to enhance your soul's progress in this lifetime. Improving your behavior and its impact upon others will diminish the chances that you will suffer some kind of negative karmic payback. The karmic number will also give you an opportunity to assess the karmic value of other people—as long as you can discover their full birth name and birth date.

To find the karmic number, add together the name number and life number. In this case, it is best to use the name on your birth certificate to obtain your name number. Then add this to the life number, which is calculated from your date of birth.

Number 1

These subjects must watch the tendency to control every-thing and to dominate others. Childhood and adolescent problems may be resolved as life progresses and ambitions can be realized, leading to material security and even wealth. They should try to balance the material and spiritual sides of everything. However, they rarely acknowledge their true spirituality and neither do they understand those who do.

Number 2

Emotional outbursts can create problems and moodiness, which can overcome logic. These people may become mar-tyrs, so they should try to be less passive. They tend to make mountains out of molehills and become upset over trivial matters. However, they are good partners who are support-ive of their families, but they must learn to make time to relax and enjoy themselves and their loved ones. They must guard against blindly trusting others, as they can attract people who are not always as honest and trustworthy as they should be.

Number 3

These individuals must guard against being conceited and boastful and they must strive to be realistic. Business ven-tures often succeed because their enthusiasm and extrav-agance makes them successful risk takers. They can be very good company, but they can sometimes spoil this by their stubborn natures, and a tendency to be envious of others and greedy where possessions and money are concerned. They are quite capable of spending their partner's money on themselves if they get the opportunity. On the plus side, they are good to their children.

Number 4

The main life lesson for these individuals is endurance through a life of uncertainty and change. They are cautious, which is no bad thing. However, they can have fixed opinions and ideas about what other people should or should not do: this can cause unnecessary problems with colleagues or relatives. They must learn self-control, consistency, and to be less complacent about their own failings.

Number 5

The life lesson for this number is perseverance and attention to detail. These honest, sincere, adaptable, and witty people lead lives full of movement and travel, either because they choose jobs that take them around the world or because they are restless. Some move from house to house or even from one country to another due to circumstances that are beyond their control.

Number 6

These people must guard against sarcasm and taking a cynical attitude. They can be condescending to others, self righteous, and possessive, but in spite of this, they tend to be popular and to have many friends. They make many sacrifices for their loved ones and others can rely on them because they have an ingrained sense of duty.

Number 7

These subjects must learn to use the many opportunities that come their way and not to give up when things go wrong. They should use their compassion and vision for the benefit of others as well as themselves, and avoid drifting into escapism. They should embrace alternative ideas and mysticism, but without becoming fanatical about these things.

Number 8

The need to learn patience is most important here and these people should guard against becoming over-materialistic. They should make an effort to create a social life and make time for fun and frivolity. They must avoid being too demanding of others or even too hard on themselves. They can hurt themselves by harboring resentments.

Number 9

These individuals often prefer their own company or the company of animals to living in a partnership. That is fine, but there are times when they must cooperate with others at work, even if they work alone. They may also need to create harmony in a family situation—even if they only have to do this at holidays or other family occasions. Their colleagues, relatives, and friends know that they can depend on them in a crisis.

Number 11

Other people may see these people as intimidating and superior, but in reality they are highly creative and blessed with enormous stamina. They rarely fail in anything they undertake, but their high principles may tip them over into obsession.

Number 22

This is a number of perfection. People with this number will happily donate their time and work for nothing for a cause they believe in, but they should learn to maintain a balance in life in order to give their idealism a realistic basis. The most positive attributes they possess are the gifts of enlightened wisdom and humanitarianism.

Predictive
Numerology

10

Numerology can be used for prediction purposes, both for long-term forecasts, as well as short-term forecasts. Here a few techniques.

(Note: the master numbers of 11 and 22 are not used in Predictive Numerology).

Simple Prediction for the Future

You can discover what any future year has in store for you simply by adding your month and day of birth to the year in question.

For example, if you were born on February 15, 1985, but you want to see what life will be like in 2020, drop the year of your birth and add the month and day to the year in question.

Then you reduce the final number to a single digit. Here is an example:

Birth date: February 15, 1985 (month 2, day 15, year 1985)
Future year: February 15, 2020 (month 2, day 15, year 2020
Addition: 2 + 1 +5 + 2 + 0 + 2 + 0 = 12
Reduction: 1 + 2 = 3

In 2020, you will be a number 3.

Use the following descriptions to see what energy and vibrations that future year will have in store for you.

Year Number 1

Number 1 indicates the start of a new cycle, so ensure that your affairs are in order. You may spend more time alone than you had in times past, so you must now examine your own needs and concentrate on making an effort to improve your circumstances. You may find yourself living in a new area, changing jobs, or making new friends now, so you must try to put the past behind you and concentrate on the future. The many changes that come your way in this future may not be easy to live with, but they will turn out for the best in the end and you will learn many new things along the way. The extra energy and drive that you have now will help you to cope with your various new situations.

Settle any outstanding matters that remain as soon as you can and you will find that during March, any uncertainty will have disappeared. Between April and November, you will be busy with new projects. Listen to what others have to say and avoid behaving in a stubborn or arrogant manner. Any new people who enter your life this year will be part of your life for some time to come, so choose partners and friends wisely.

Year Number 2

It is not a good idea to take major decisions this future year, but you should keep the resolutions that you made in your past. Things may not seem to be moving fast enough for your liking, so try to develop patience and to establish basic harmony in your life. You will need to take other people into account and to work with them rather than against them. This means developing tact and diplomacy. Other people may have their own ideas and they may not wish to change them.

This should be a year of good health and you can expect some opportunities for travel. There may be some difficulties to face in your love life, but you should work hard to improve this if it is at all possible. Indeed, you must work hard to establish partnerships of many kinds this year.

If you fancy a change of address, it would be wiser to wait until next year. It is possible that you will decide to take up a new creative activity this year, and if this is the case, it may assume importance in years to come. Whatever your long term aims are, keep them on track, but try to take some time off and to relax whenever the chance presents itself.

Year Number 3

You may reap the rewards of past efforts and you could even expect a windfall or two in this year; even a gamble might pay off. Do not allow setbacks or negative and envious people to spoil things for you. You will be busy and you might even find yourself in the public eye at some point. A burst of creativity could bring new opportunities. Take them—you should be full of enthusiasm and feeling optimistic. You can have a very productive and happy year if you are determined to make the best of everything.

If you are single, you can expect social gatherings, happiness, fun, and romance to come your way. This year, all partnerships and friendships are well starred. Maybe you will decide it is time for a new image, so keep a careful eye on your diet and brush up your appearance and your wardrobe.

Year Number 4

Material needs are important this year, so get down to business and work hard. Set yourself targets or goals and ensure that you do all you can to reach these. This is not the year in which to put too much energy or time into your social life. Lay the foundations for the future by making plans, clearing away anything that wastes your time and energy, and prepare to start afresh.

You will find yourself thinking about money as you may well have a number of unexpected expenses. Be careful to save whenever you have the opportunity because financial stability will be important, but do not become greedy or obsessed by money concerns.

Your home will be the focus of much of your attention and you may make long needed improvements there. Alternatively, you may arrange or rearrange your mortgage or some other loan for home improvements or extensions. The increase in your career status and earning power might be at the back of this, as you will now be in a position to improve your living quarters. The summer months will show progress in all your affairs, so you will need to be patient and you will need to keep an eye on health matters.

Year Number 5

This is a year of movement in your affairs. If there is something in your life that is not working, this is the time to change it, so you may buy a new house, change your job, or travel, but you must think any decisions through carefully. Luck will come your way during the middle part of the year, so go ahead and follow that luck and don't allow others to hold you back.

This is the number of communication, so you will have a full schedule, many meetings, telephone calls, emails, and invitations. A potential love interest will find you attractive and interesting, so all the activity will make you feel as if you are in a whirlwind. Go everywhere, meet everyone, and experience everything this year. People will take notice of you. You may start some new venture or get a promotion at work.

Expect the unexpected throughout the year and remember to take every new opportunity and chance for advancement.

Year Number 6

The main emphasis this year is on your personal affairs, so you must attend to any domestic and emotional issues that are outstanding. You may experience matrimonial problems or difficulties with friends, or perhaps there are outstanding legal matters to be resolved. Any friendships that have been under a cloud will improve during this year.

If you have been struggling to make a dicey friendship or a love relationship work, you will realize that you can do nothing more to improve it. This means that you may lose a friend or give up on a bad relationship for good. Whether this is the case or not, if you are alone, you could meet someone new, because you will want to be content and settled. The greatest issues are related to balance and harmony and this is a very important year for love.

Year Number 7

Step back this year and have a period of relaxation and rest. This will give you a chance to take stock of your life and consider yourself more than you normally do. Concentrate your energy on your own welfare, and, for once, take care of your own health and requirements before those of others. Put yourself first. A short spell away on your own or periods of meditation may be what you need this year.

Travel is highlighted this year, so you will find yourself taking short trips. If your work involves travel or if it concerns the travel industry, you can expect to have an especially good year. Unexpected opportunities for travel may take you by surprise and they will allow you the opportunities you need to learn new things.

Do not spend too much time worrying about the material aspects of your life this year, because this is a time for philosophical or spiritual issues. Do not be surprised to discover a new interest in mysticism, magic, and spirituality. If you are already working in this field, this will be an extremely rewarding year. Even if such matters are of no interest to you, you may find yourself spending more of your time and energy helping others throughout the year.

Year Number 8

Rewards for past efforts will become apparent during this year and although they may be slow to arrive, they will eventually come along. You can expect financial and business successes. Advancement of all kinds and promotion at work are highlighted throughout the year.

If in the past you have been unwise or reckless, those decisions—good or bad—will catch up with you. You may experience losses and a new feeling of instability. You might receive a welcome windfall, but it is equally possible that you will lose your job or have financial problems. You will win and lose in the game of life this year.

Elderly relatives may become more part of your life and older people in general can find that they have important roles to fulfill. Property matters will be important—many people may be involved in buying or selling property, possibly in connection with older relatives.

Romantic issues come to the forefront, as this is an important emotional year. Some would call this a karmic year.

Year Number 9

For many people, this last year in the cycle will be a time of reflection, so you will look at your situation and assess those things that you really need to change. You will also start to look at ways of improving your position or making personal strides in both practical terms and spiritual ones. Having said this, you may not be able to implement these changes or improvements until next year, because this is a time for consolidation or preparation rather than for change.

Do not be surprised to discover yourself acting impulsively and feeling that you must make some decisions quickly this year. However, take care to consider all your options so that you do not regret later what you have done; it is likely that your judgment is not at its best. This is not the time to make drastic changes to your personal life and it is important to try to retain a sense of balance.

Make plans for the future, reflect on what you have achieved, and spend time thinking carefully. Things that are no longer relevant will start to slide away this year. You could feel depressed and insecure at times, but without this knowledge and understanding, you cannot begin the year that follows this one with a clean slate.

Think less of the past and more about the future. If you can view the year in terms of progress in the future rather than endings and loss in the present, you will discover that many of the events that are happening will turn out to be for the best. The solid friendships you have built over past years will be important to you this year and you should show your partner and friends jut how much you value them. Do not become over-sensitive or obsessive or lose your sense of perspective.

Short Term Forecasts

Here are some quick and easy ways to work out your personal vibration for any future month, week, day, or even any hour.

Reduce your birth date to a single number—your life number. Then add that number to the number of upcoming month, day, or hour in order to examine the forecast.

(Note: the master numbers 11 and 22 are not used in this method.)

Months

Add your life number to the number of the month. For example, if your life number is 6, and you want a quick forecast for the coming month of September (month 9):

Add 6 and 9

Combine and reduce to 15

Reduce to a single digit: the result is 6

Your prediction number is 6

Days

Add your life number to the day of the month. Thus if your life number is 1 and the day you want to look at is the 18th, this is

1 + 1 + 8

The result is 10

Combine and reduce to 1

Your prediction number is 1

Hours

Use a 24-hour clock (where noon is 12 and midnight is 24) and add your life number to the time. Therefore, if your life number is 4 and you want to see what will happen at 7 o'clock in the evening (which is hour 19), you will add

4 + 1 + 9

The result is 14

Combine and reduce to 5

Your prediction number is 5

Now you can look up your short-term prediction number to see what is likely to happen.

Prediction Number 1

The vibration of Number 1 brings opportunities for a fresh start. If you need to tackle something difficult, you will have the energy and optimism with which to do it. This is a good time to sign a contract, finalize an agreement, or start a project. This is also a good day for chatting with interesting and intelligent people and getting some input and ideas from them. You will not be short of positive ideas, but you must analyze them to see if they will hold water. Avoid haste and impetuosity if you can, and try not to walk all over other people.

Prediction Number 2

This is a good time for continuing a project and to consolidate what you have done so far. This is also an excellent time to mingle and cooperate with others, to listen to what they have to say, or to seek help from them if you need it. Partnership issues should go well, but sometimes a the energy of Number 2 is a time of conflict, or a period during which you should put more care into expressing yourself in a calm, reasonable manner. Try to find time to relax a little during the course of this period if you can.

Prediction Number 3

This is an excellent time for creative thinking and for coming up with problem-solving ideas. If you are pursue artistic matters, these will go well. You should avoid behaving in an obstinate or irritable manner with others, and if you need to stand up to unpleasant people, you should try to do this in a direct and assertive manner and avoid seeming overly stubborn. This should be a great time for parties or socializing. If you can do something other than work, do so now. If you need to schedule a meeting or a discussion, or if you need to take a short trip or go shopping, this is a good time for such activities.

Prediction Number 4

This is an excellent time during which to get jobs done in a practical and constructive manner. If a project requires special effort or if it requires special attention to specific details, do it now. This is not such a great time to start a new project, but you will be able to break the back of one that has been hanging around for a while. You should also reach out to all those who you have to deal with or cooperate with, and to pay attention to personal relationships and partnerships. The only problem is that you might ride a little roughshod over others in your haste to accomplish everything.

Prediction Number 5

Number 5 times are particularly changeable, so you may choose to change direction now and to try something new. It is no good making plans, because you will need to go with the flow at this time. Short journeys or even longer trips could well be in the cards during this spell. You could meet interesting people, or find yourself having new and different experiences. Phone calls, emails, or letters could take you by surprise, but in general, all matters regarding communication will go well. Try teaching someone how to do something, or learn something new yourself at this time.

Prediction Number 6

Despite the fact that this number is often associated with quite hard work, there is evidence that you will be able to take some time off in order to do some of the more fun kinds of shopping. By this, I mean shopping for something other than food or other basic items—treat yourself! Listen to the music you like and do the things that make you happy. This is a good time for love and affairs of the heart. Nevertheless, work will take precedence during some part of this period, as will doing things for your loved ones.

Prediction Number 7

Matters concerning love, passion, affairs of the heart, and relationships come to the forefront now. Concentrate on your love relationships today if you can, even if it means neglecting some of your chores, because there will be something in your personal life that needs attention. This is also an excellent time during which to go on an inward journey and to do some thinking or to contemplate spiritual matters. If you have any studying or research to do, this is the time for it. Try to use some part of this rather quiet period for a little relaxation.

Prediction Number 8

Financial and business matters rule when this number is in operation, so if you need to sort out your finances, pay bills, and reconcile your checkbook, get down to this now. Business matters will flourish and if you need help or advice from those in positions of authority, this is the time to ask for it. In addition, you may be able to resolve a financial problem. Your intuition will be spot-on, so you can sit back, observe others for a while and try to fathom out their underlying motives and agendas. At this time, you might prefer to spend some time alone. One source of ancient wisdom says that if you are likely to hear of a death, it will be on a Number 8 day.

Prediction Number 9

This is a good time to end a cycle of events and bring jobs or certain aspects of your recent life to completion. You may want to look back on what you have achieved and make plans for the future, but you cannot start anything new just yet. It would be best to avoid taking action or making specific decisions on a Number 9 period if possible. Finish any outstanding jobs and get ready for the action to start again later. If there is nothing much going on in your life or at work, use this time to clear out cupboards, sort through your paperwork and throw away out-of-date stuff that is cluttering up your space. A specific piece of advice for this period is to be honest and fair in all your dealings with others.

Working backward

Because many of the above descriptions focus on certain outcomes, it is possible to work backward if you want to schedule your time around a specific desired outcome.

Let's say you have a big exam coming up. We've seen that the vibration of Number 7 is particularly beneficial for this. The reverse method is simple: as an example, if your life number is 8, you'll need to add it to something that results in a 7. Adding another 8 to it (hour 8, hour 17, day 8, day 17 are a few examples) with give you 16, which will reduce to 7.

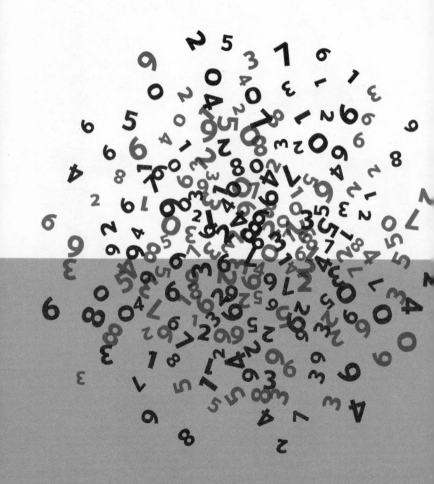

Numerology
and
Relationships

11

This chapter is mainly about love relationships. This may include an enduring marriage, a long-term friendship, a passionate fling, and passing fancy. Some combinations are good for a relationship in work or business—after all, the best business ventures are those we love—so I have included a few of these as well. This overview is for both women and men who want to give their partners (or potential partners) a critical once-over.

The number of stars after each number shows the most successful partnerships, but even those with few stars can work. Sometimes opposites attract, and relationships that don't appear at first glance to have any potential can work out. Only those with no stars at all have no real chance of anything more than a short-term fling.

For this system, first calculate your name number. Use the name that you usually go by, which will more than likely be a shortened version of your birth name (for example, Suzie Collins for Susannah Sophia Collins*). Then do the same calculation for the person with whom you are considering a relationship.

Find your name number in the headings below. Under these headings you will find a list that corresponds to your partner's

name number. You'll notice the numbers are not in consecutive order; they are ordered from best relationship match (four stars) to least (zero stars).

*A random, imaginary name, not meant to represent any real person living or dead.

Number 1

3 ★ ★ ★ ★

You share enthusiasm and a determination to succeed; while you will compete with each other, you will also enjoy lots of passionate lovemaking. You would also have many good laughs together.

4 ★ ★ ★ ★

This works as both of you are practical, logical, and keen on keeping up appearances; however, you may want a family and your partner may run a mile from the idea of being part of a family unit.

7 ★ ★ ★ ★

You both share an interest in setting clear limits and you share an appreciation in the outdoors, nature, and the romance of wild places, so you would both enjoy energetic outdoorsy pastimes.

22 ★ ★ ★ ★

Although 22 is a dreamer and you are a "doer," the potential for a long-term bond is excellent as long as you give each other the space that you both need.

1 ★ ★ ★

This relationship promises lots of fun as you are both creative and passionate, but since you would both want to take charge of every situation, so there might be one too many clashes here for a long-term romance.

8 ★ ★ ★

You will appreciate this hard-working partner who takes responsibility and who can handle success, but you both like to be in charge, so it may not work out in the long run.

5 ★ ★

On one hand, your hard-working partner will be happy to spend hours chatting with you, but this partner needs the thrill of the chase, so this might only work as a short-term attraction.

6 ★ ★

Number 6s love to make their partner happy, but they prefer staying at home to going out and making their mark in the world, and this isn't your idea of fun.

9 ★

Both of you are impatient, but you are both loyal and strong in a crisis. There is little chance of a successful love connection, but a working arrangement might succeed, as there is a measure of mutual respect.

2

This relationship would emphasize too many differences, so it is best avoided.

11

An attraction is unlikely; this would work neither in love or business.

Number 2

5 ★ ★ ★ ★

You both love to chat, debate, talk about what you read or see on the television, and to gossip, so you would never have time to become bored with each other.

8 ★ ★ ★ ★

You respect this person's serious attitude to work and to making a success of things. You will help your partner to achieve success and you would then both enjoy spending your partner's money.

2 ★ ★ ★

Lots of fun and passion are the keys to combining with these naturally attractive people. There may be an element of competition in this relationship.

9 ★ ★ ★

This combination makes loving partners and both can be a tower of strength in a crisis. You could be passionate lovers, as long as the association includes work or business as well as romance.

11 ★ ★ ★

This link works well as long as you both give plenty of time to it. Each of you has high ideals that you hate to compromise. Your shared interests and passion for life—and for each other—will make this one a success.

22 ★ ★ ★

You both have many admirers and both are usually successful in all kinds of relationships. This could be great fun with lots of passionate moments.

6 ★ ★

You are both loving and faithful, but there is a great deal of emphasis on both of you looking good, so there may be clashes about who spends what on their appearance.

7 ★ ★

You will appreciate your partner's loving nature, but you may not be able to cope with the mood swings. Attraction will not be enough to sustain a long-term bond.

1 ★

These people always want to be in charge and there are just too many differences to create a good relationship.

3 ★

Although your partner would do his or her best to make this succeed, a tendency to be flirtatious would upset you.

4

You want family life but this partner isn't interested, so no chance here.

Number 3

6 ★ ★ ★ ★

This would make a stunning affair, but you have a traditional attitude to marriage, while your partner does not. An excellent business combination though, as you would set the pace and your partner would deliver the goods.

9 ★ ★ ★ ★

You are both loyal and you both enjoy variety and change, so there are good possibilities for a successful long-term link.

1 ★ ★ ★

This person wants to be the head of a family and the center of attention. This can be a fun romance with lots of passion, but you would eventually become fed up at having to play the part of an admiring audience.

3 ★ ★ ★

You share the same sense of humor and need for affection, so this can be a passionate and successful choice. You would give each other the space that you need.

5 ★ ★ ★

Although loving the thrill of the chase, this partner will work hard to make a relationship succeed. You share an interest in reading, thinking, talking, and traveling, so you would certainly have a fun time together.

7 ★ ★

Although this partner is renowned for moodiness, he or she wants to love and be loved, but his weird attitude will leave you wondering. There is an attraction, but is it enough?

8 ★ ★

Home life seems to come in second place unless this combines romance with work or business. There could be a clash of personalities.

2 ★

You may feel stifled by a partner who fusses, hovers over you, and restricts your freedom. Too many differences suggest little chance of a successful partnership.

4 ★

If this partner wants to marry you, it is because you fit into a particular pattern that he or she has in mind. Is this person after you for your house or your money? Maybe not, but the possibility exists.

11 ★

You need attention and you need to feel as if you are in charge, and this person won't give you enough attention or allow you to make decisions.

22

You will want to get out of this one almost before you get into it, but 22 will cling, so it is best not to get involved in the first place.

Number 4

1 ★ ★ ★ ★

You can manage this sexy, passionate person and the opposites in your natures will always keep each of you interested, so this has excellent long-term possibilities.

4 ★ ★ ★ ★

Two number 4s could hit it off well together, since neither enters into a long-term relationship lightly. Your mutual love of method, system, and efficiency might drive other people mad, but you understand each other perfectly.

7 ★ ★ ★ ★

Renowned for their mood swings, these attractive, physical, sexy people may puzzle you, but as long as you give each other loads of space, this can work well.

2 ★ ★ ★

This will work as long as your partner doesn't try to crowd you or control you, but the passion that you share will make this a fun event—even if only a short term one.

6 ★ ★ ★

Loving, faithful, and successful, these people put their energy into making money, which suits you perfectly. You could have lots of fun together amassing a fortune. This would also work as a business relationship.

11 ★ ★ ★

Given time to concentrate on the bond between you, and bearing in mind that your partner might be a control freak, this could work out well. Healthy competition would create a fun-filled, passionate romance.

22 ★ ★ ★

Although your partner will have his or her head turned by too many other admirers, the passion between you could keep the spark alive. A useful working partnership.

8 ★ ★

This entrepreneurial type is well organized, but frequently intolerant and cold in a close relationship. The clash of personalities will soon send you off to find true love and affection elsewhere.

9 ★ ★

Loyal, faithful, good in a crisis, and capable of making split-second decisions; however, this partner wants everything now! Attractive, maybe, but this looks more likely as a working arrangement.

3 ★

You might appreciate this person's sense of humor, but little else, and you have little in common. This works best when it is nothing more than a casual friendship.

6

What on earth would you find to talk about?

Number 5

2 ★ ★ ★ ★

This can be a successful and passionate long-term link as long as your partner doesn't patronize you or hem you in. A Number 2 means well and is loving and loyal.

8 ★ ★ ★ ★

Your partner is a responsible, successful individual who can make you very happy and contented, especially if you share an interest in business. Excellent possibilities for an enduring situation.

11 ★ ★ ★ ★

You are both excellent communicators who are both willing to put the effort into learning how to make a long-term bond successful. Provided career matters do not take first place, this is a good bet for both partners.

3 ★ ★ ★

Although they love an audience, these subjects will do their best to make a partner happy in the security of a long-term permanent connection. If they feel loved and cherished, they bring a sense of fun and passion into this link.

5 ★ ★ ★

A strong sex drive makes for a passionate relationship with lots of laughs. Both of you are romantic and addicted to travel, so this is well worth putting some effort into.

7 ★ ★ ★

In spite of the initial attraction, take care not to allow your partner to draw you into competitive power struggles and spoil the chances of long-term success. If you share the same interests, that will help you along.

1 ★ ★

Your partner is demanding, bossy, creative, sexy, and passionate. If you don't mind the fact that he or she may be having flings outside the relationship, and if you are willing to play second fiddle, that's fine. Otherwise, avoid this clash of personalities if you are looking for a long-term situation.

9 ★ ★

This partner is loyal and passionate, but can be impatient and rash, while thinking that he or she is actually sensible and well organized. Do you want such a challenge? There could be a bad personality clash here.

4 ★

Faithful and predictable in love, this may just be another control freak in the making. Attractive, perhaps, but remember that these people often marry for money or remain single all their lives.

6 ★

This partner can be a perfectionist taskmaster who fails to notice when a partner needs love and affection. Very little chance of a successful long-term romance.

22 ★

Although this may be the ideal faithful partner at first glance, their personal magnetism attracts too much attention from others. Do you want to spend the rest of your life being sidelined by a crowd of admirers with someone who wants freedom, but who also refuses to let you go?

Number 6

3 ★ ★ ★ ★

You stick to a partner and this person needs that, so you can give each other the reassurance that you both need. Your partner's fantastic sense of humor and desire to make you happy will make for an enduring love relationship.

5 ★ ★ ★ ★

If you and your partner are at a stage in life when you are both prepared to settle down with one person, this will work. You will have loads to talk about and many shared hobbies and interests. Otherwise, this would make a great loving friendship. It would work well on a business basis too.

4 ★ ★ ★

This loyal partner is a tower of strength in a crisis. He or she loves challenge and variety, and this also works for you, but you may feel harassed at times because this individual hates to be kept waiting.

6 ★ ★ ★

Two number 6 people together will understand each other instinctively. They will work hard to create a loving and faithful partnership with lots of passion and just a hint of competitiveness. However, both can become very downhearted on occasion, so each of you would have to prop the other up at times.

8 ★ ★ ★

Combine this personal association with work or a business and it will be successful. Both partners will be happy and content with equal responsibility for the love and passion that makes a romance fizz.

1 ★ ★

Number 1 people love being the head of a large family. If that's not what you want in a partner, you should avoid this person, who always needs to be in the limelight and at the center of attention.

2 ★ ★

You may feel stifled by the attentiveness of a Number 2 person who is always loving and concerned for the family and those who rely on him or her. It is likely that a clash of personalities could emerge, which would make you both unhappy in the end.

11 ★ ★

Because they love to be in control, these people have a lot to learn about one-on-one situations. Although you may be mutually attracted, you would probably resent your partner's need to put a career before all else.

7 ★

This person's real goal is to save the planet and he or she is happier with a group of like-minded friends than in a close relationship. Although warm and caring, this person makes a better friend than marriage-type partner.

9 ★

This can make a great working arrangement, as your partner would think up the ideas for you to carry out, but it would make an exhausting love partnership.

22

This clever and creative person has great potential for success as long as he or she is alongside someone who can pick up the pieces when some of the ideas fail. As a romantic attachment, you would soon get each other down.

Number 7

1 ★ ★ ★ ★

You are so different that you could fit together very well in a way, as each of you will complement the other. Your partner is a natural leader while you are an idealistic dreamer, but both of you are creative, sexy, and passionate.

4 ★ ★ ★ ★

Although they often prefer to remain single, there are good possibilities for a successful relationship with this individual, who loves to be involved in the community and is passionate about animals. This is someone who will be faithful and predictable.

7 ★ ★ ★ ★

These two people will instinctively understand each other, which is a good start in any partnership. Fun and passion, along with many shared interests, make this a good link.

22 ★ ★ ★ ★

This person has exceptional talents and abilities and you would appreciate this. In spite of having many admirers, they will remain faithful to one partner. You are unlikely to resist their charm. An excellent possibility for a long-term bond.

5 ★ ★ ★

Although they hate to be restricted, in a partnership with Number 7, this is unlikely to be an issue. You both love to travel, enjoy romance, and share a strong sex drive. A fun relationship with lots of laughs and long-term potential.

9 ★ ★ ★

This might be fun on a short-term basis, but you like to go with the flow while your partner wants to do everything yesterday, so you would soon get on each other's nerves. However, your mutual love of variety and challenge brings spice into this relationship, so despite the odds, this has a good chance of lasting.

2 ★ ★

This could work in its own strange way—say, if you both took up an interest in alternative therapies and psychic matters, otherwise you might find your partner a little too conventional for your tastes. However, you will appreciate your partner's passion.

3 ★ ★

Your partner would demand more attention than you want to give, so in spite of a mutual attraction at first, this is unlikely to work out. In addition, this partner is surprisingly flirtatious and this may not work in a permanent situation.

11 ★ ★

You both have high ideals and neither of you can compromise, so you both have a lot to learn about how to make a relationship work. Power gives this partner a kick because he or she needs to be in control. This is unlikely to be a workable partnership.

6 ★

You prefer to go with the flow while this partner needs to focus on details and expediency. Although these people love to make others happy, this would not be a comfortable relationship for either of you, in spite of a superficial attraction.

8 ★

Only a relationship that includes work or business has any chance of success.

Number 8

2 ★ ★ ★ ★

You are ambitious and you focus on your career while this partner is oriented towards looking after the home and family. This could be a wonderful combination, as you would each have a defined role—you as the breadwinner and your partner as the homemaker. More importantly, you can keep your thoughts and feelings to yourself whenever your partner gets into a state and loses his temper.

5 ★ ★ ★ ★

This lover's amazing sex drive, love of travel, and preference for short-term projects makes them great fun. An excellent communicator, he or she will work hard at a keeping love alive, so this is a good bet for a demanding person like you. There is every possibility of a highly successful long-term relationship here.

11 ★ ★ ★ ★

Good at making friends, career minded, and interested in the media world, these people often work in films or TV. They have the highest ideals and are willing to learn how to manage love and marriage, as they can focus on a partner's needs. This is an ideal mate for you.

1 ★ ★ ★

Even if they sometimes behave like tyrants, these people are irresistible, especially to ambitious Number 8 who needs strong a partner to manage his family life. This highly creative, sexy, passionate lover could be an ideal choice.

6 ★ ★ ★

The genuine ability to make a partner happy makes these attractive individuals loyal long-term partners. Perhaps not always traditionalists where marriage is concerned, but you may appreciate that, especially as there would be plenty of fun, passion, and a hint of competition.

8 ★ ★ ★

This makes a wonderful business arrangement as long as you each have your own sphere of activity and don't compete with each other. As partners, you must each have your own career interests, but when you are not at work, you will have an instinctive understanding, many laughs and many passionate moments.

3 ★ ★

Bright, cheerful, and enthusiastic, this partner is determined to succeed. He or she may be both pushy and flirtatious at the start of a relationship. Although you both start out with the best of intentions, there may be a clash of personalities, which bodes ill for the long term.

4 ★ ★

If you are both into farming, horses, running a kennels, and that kind of thing, you could certainly work well together, but there is not enough to sustain a loving bond between you.

22 ★ ★

In spite of an initial magnetism, these individuals are concerned to get ahead in a career. A short-term business venture will work because you have the financial acumen and your colleague has the practical knowledge that you can use. As a romance, this would not last more than five minutes.

7 ★

You are on two different planets. This person is emotional, dreamy, and happy to live and work in a somewhat chaotic environment, and all that would drive you nuts. There is little chance of a long-term relationship being successful.

9

These people would rather be one of a group than make sacrifices for their partners.

Number 9

3 ★ ★ ★ ★

You both love doing things spontaneously, and you both think on your feet and move very quickly. You appreciate each other's efficiency at home and in business. Your partner will make every effort to make you happy, and while a little flirtatious, in the security of a loving bond, this may not be an issue.

6 ★ ★ ★ ★

Your partner is only really happy and secure when in a loving relationship and number 6's perfectionist tendencies would not upset or bother you. Indeed, you could concentrate on your career in the knowledge that your partner is taking good care of the family, the home, and your possessions.

2 ★ ★ ★

Well balanced and level headed, these protective, tactful individuals can create an atmosphere of calm and contentment, but this link could also be amusing and full of zest with just a hint of competition.

7 ★ ★ ★

You will find this loving person ideal as long as you give him or her space for their many outside interests. Your partner may be moody sometimes, but is attractive and sexy, so this could be a passionate affair that can stand the test of time.

9 ★ ★ ★

You may both appear to be rash and impatient to outsiders, but you understand each other perfectly in a long-term committed partnership. Both are loyal and you both have the kind of backbone that enables you to cope with any crisis. You might both enjoy working together in a capacity where you need to cope with anything that can happen.

11 ★ ★ ★

Communication is the key to success in loving relationships and you each have something important to contribute. You may seek to compete with each other at times, but this should not prove an insurmountable problem for either partner.

4 ★ ★

Although they make wonderful employees, be aware that these number 4s are loners. They often prefer not to make committed relationships—except with their pets. There may be passion and fun at first, but this is probably not going to turn into a satisfying long-term partnership.

5 ★ ★

It is important to understand that these people can easily become restless, so if you want your partner to stay behind while you follow your pursuits outside, you will come home one day and find your dinner in the oven, but nobody home!

22 ★ ★

If you like to have someone with whom to share an occasional vacation or to help you out when you have a sticky problem to discuss at work, you will become friends. Otherwise, there is little to keep either of you interested.

1 ★

The moment that this powerful and self-centered personality starts laying the law down to you is the moment that you leave, so there is little chance of success.

8

This partner will snap at you and expect you to take this. You may put up with this once, but when it happens again, you will vanish into the mist.

Number 11

5 ★ ★ ★ ★

You share an interest in travel, people, education, and keeping your minds active. You will respect your partner's skill in do-it-yourself activities and devotion to career. Add a sexual attraction to this and you have a good chance of making this work.

8 ★ ★ ★ ★

These ambitious people are not easy to live with, but you have what it takes to make this bond work. For one thing, you are both creative and capable in your different ways, so you will always have some kind of project to talk about. This would also make an excellent business relationship.

2 ★ ★ ★

This loving and caring personality is also levelheaded, balanced, and diplomatic. If you share hobbies and interests and have lots to talk about, this makes a great association that has a strong element of friendship as well as love.

9 ★ ★ ★

Although these people like to be part of a group, they understand the importance of personal love and commitment and they will make extremely generous long-term partners.

11 ★ ★ ★

You both have an oddball side to you, and as long as your interests are similar, you would get along very nicely. Although competitive, this person is lively and passionate, loving and appreciative of family life, so it would work well.

22 ★ ★ ★

This person has probably had a difficult childhood, so he or she will appreciate being in a close and loving relationship. This person is generous and kind-hearted, so occasional outbursts of temper or silliness won't upset you.

4 ★ ★

A combination of these numbers will make a successful business partnership if you deal with the creative or manufacturing side of things, and your partner handles the bookkeeping and finances. In a personal relationship, the lack of passion or real interest in each other makes it a non-starter.

6 ★ ★

Here is a hard taskmaster who expects his or her partner to channel a lot of energy into making money. Although number 6s love to make others happy, there is every chance that they will put their career first and may not notice when a partner needs some love and affection. There is, out there, a better partner for you.

7 ★ ★

Although these people make loving partners, and they are sexy, attractive, and physical, their frequent mood swings may leave you wondering just how important the relationship really is. Not an ideal choice.

1 ★

This would make a dynamic business partnership, although even here, you would both fight for supremacy. You are both so focused on your career aims that a personal relationship is almost impossible to imagine.

3 ★

Because they often feel lonely even in a close loving relationship, these subjects can be flirtatious and needy. This is not a good partner for you as the link would fall apart the moment you tried to regain your power in the situation by controlling your partner.

Number 22

1 ★ ★ ★ ★

Always in charge, sexy and passionate in close relationships, this can be an excellent choice of partner. They are never be tempted to stray from a long-term commitment or to indulge in affairs outside a marriage. It is not a problem for you that this charismatic, creative individual demands to be center stage and sometimes behaves like a tyrant. This has the making of a first class, long term relationship.

7 ★ ★ ★ ★

Although it might seem that dreams of saving the planet or adopting a cause, or embracing mysticism and philosophy are most important for this partner, he or she is loving and kind; this may work surprisingly well on all levels. A good choice that should bring happiness.

2 ★ ★ ★

You are both interested in having a partner and in family life, so there is much potential here. Even if you fill the house with stray dogs and children, your partner may grumble, but will be happy enough as long as he or she has a personal workshop or space to design things and contentedly fiddle around.

6 ★ ★ ★

This person will go a long way to make you happy and content. Loving and faithful, the most they demand is that their partner doesn't turn the house into a mess; this person is concerned with appearances, both in home and personal dress. There could be much worse to live up to.

11 ★ ★ ★

Good communicators, excellent teachers and writers, Number 11s make influential friends easily and will put effort into making a relationship work and they will appreciate the clever way that you make the house and garden look good.

4 ★ ★

You need far more reassurance than this person can give you. Number 4 would make a fine friend and a good work mate, but nothing more, really.

8 ★ ★

You need love, attention, affection, and reassurance, but this person is too busy building an empire somewhere to have the time or patience to devote to your needs. He or she just cannot sit down and listen to you while you talk about your feelings. This is not an ideal partnership.

9 ★ ★

This person is something of a loner, and won't understand your need for a close relationship; there will be no emotional support when your self-confidence takes a nosedive. You may appreciate the company during a holiday romance, but not when it comes down to living together.

3 ★

These people are too needy to be able to maintain a successful relationship with 22. Don't even bother trying; it will end in tears all round.

5 ★

This person looks sexy and attractive at first glance, but may not be ready to give up having a good time and to settle down with one partner and maintain a marriage or committed relationship.

22

Although there will be some basic understanding here and possibly even initial attraction, this is a recipe for a personality clash that is likely to be horrific. So, unless you like to have a really good argument every single day, find someone else.

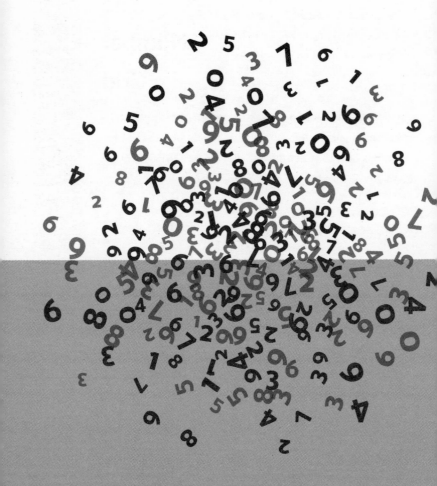

The
Number
Grid

12

The number grid is a Pythagorean construct. It can be used in many ways, but I will show you the simplest method for using the number grid.

This grid adds a little something extra to your reading—deeper meaning, or more insight for example—and for this, you should use your life number or destiny number; that is, the number that you get from your date of your birth.

Each row of numbers has a particular energy when you read the columns vertically and horizontally.

	Physical	Intellectual	Spiritual
Creativity	3	6	9
Emotion	2	5	8
Material	1	4	7

The Key to the Grid

The first vertical row (1, 2, 3) relates to the physical body.

The middle vertical row (4, 5, 6) relates to the intellect.

The last vertical row (7, 8, 9) relates to the spiritual nature.

The bottom horizontal row (1, 4, 7) relates to the material world.

The middle horizontal row (2, 5, 8) relates to the emotions.

The top horizontal row (3, 6, 9) relates to creativity.

Diagonal line (1, 5, 9) relates to communication.

Diagonal line (3, 5, 7) relates to effectiveness.

Individual Numbers

Each number has a meaning of its own. You have already seen these ideas expressed in the first chapter on single numbers, but now you can see how they work out, both singly, and as part of the grid.

1   Personal creativity

2   Feelings

3   Resources

4   Instincts and logic

5   Expansion and senses

6   Intuition and theory

7   Setting limits

8   Transformation

9   Spiritual creativity

Interpreting the Grid

Check out the vertical, horizontal and/or diagonal lines that contain your number.

Vertical line 1, 2, 3

These numbers describe the physical world, so these individuals know their identity; they can feel with the conscious mind and can perform actions.

Vertical line 4, 5, 6

The numbers describe the world of the intellect, abstract thinking, creative thought, imagination and theory.

Vertical line 7, 8, 9

These numbers describe the world of the spirit. They relate to the unconscious mind and spiritually creative talents with which the subject has been endowed.

Horizontal line 1, 4, 7

These numbers are associated with the material world, so they focus on thinking things through logically and getting them done in a practical and realistic way.

Horizontal line 2, 5, 8

These numbers focus on emotions, the unconscious mind, the feelings and intuition.

Horizontal line 3, 6, 9

These numbers concern creativity so a touch of genius—or at least great creative talent—might be indicated. These numbers also refer to karmic rewards from previous lives.

Diagonal line 1, 5, 9

These emphasize the value of communications, a willingness to learn, expansion and use of talents, spiritual creativity and the ability to create new life.

Diagonal line 3, 5, 7

These numbers denote the ability to act sensibly, and a desire to learn and to understand how to set limits.

Numerology
for Other
Purposes

13

A friend of mine married for a second time and her husband told her that every automobile he had ever owned had a registration number that added up to a 3, 6, or 9. This didn't include the letters on the number plate, just the numbers. He hadn't deliberately chosen cars with these numbers, it had just happened. Since they have been together, they have owned various second-hand vehicles, and at one time, they even inherited one from a relative who died. Sure enough, every single car that her husband drove had a registration number that added up to 3, 6, or 9—even the inherited one!

This phenomenon is not as uncommon as one would think. There are people who seem to be followed around by a certain number; most often people come to see this as their lucky number. There doesn't seem to be any rhyme or reason for this, as these numbers are not prominent in their numerology, astrology, or any other system—they just appear to exist for some weird reason of their own.

Houses and Addresses

It is interesting to see how your house number might affect your life, and the same goes for a business address. This is a brief rundown of the energies of each number from 1 to 9. Naturally, if your number is longer than a single digit (and, of course, most are) you must add the numbers together and then reduce them to a single digit in the usual way.

Number	House Number Interpretation
1	A fresh start, a new lifestyle, independence and self-starting, also getting a concept or business off the ground
2	Partnerships, relationships, cooperating with others in private life and in business
3	Creativity, childbirth, passion, but also arguments. Good for business enterprises
4	Consolidation, family life, earning and saving money, putting down roots in a marriage or a business
5	Movement, travel, visits, visitors and plenty of conversation. In business, marketing and communication take precedence.
6	A new relationship, making a new home for someone you love, successful work, and a need to be on top of everything. In business, sometimes too much to do.
7	Great for a holiday home or place in which to relax, meditate, or develop psychically. Not good for business—too vague and nebulous.
8	Money will pile up here, but only after a period of hard work. Even if you are no businessperson, you will become one here.
9	You will stay here long enough to bring a relationship or child rearing to an end. This number encourages you to keep going until it is time for a new phase to begin—then you will move and change your address again.

Vehicles

So now, let us take an amusing look at your automobile, van, truck, or motorcycle number. First, ignoring any letters, reduce the registration to a single digit.

Number	Vehicle Interpretation
1	This vehicle's number is fast and reckless, so watch out for speeding tickets
2	Two likes company, so you will rarely be alone when driving this automobile
3	You will think up creative ideas while driving this vehicle, but difficulty in diagnosing faults will be an ongoing problem
4	A stately, respectable, but boring vehicle that will last forever—your mother will be happy that you are in a safe car
5	This sporty number longs to move, so you will spend more time driving than before
6	Shopping, chores, carting children about, and giving lifts to neighbors and relatives characterizes this workhorse
7	Keep your mind on the road and listen to lively music, because this vehicle could put you in a trance
8	This is a really hot number, so your automobile is either a prestige sporty vehicle—or it just thinks it is
9	You will put up with this dreadful old lemon while working your butt off to save for something better

Entertainment, Business, and Success

For the most part, numerology works with the name or number that you were given at birth, although in this book, I advocate using the name you use in daily life for some of the interpretations. However, what should you do when you need to make up a name for a particular purpose? What if you desire success as an actor? What if you desire to write under a *nom de plume*? What if you need to come up with a name for a new business? Why not choose something that works? Here are a few ideas.

Businesses take time to get off the ground if they add up to a Number 8, but they will stand the test of time. A Number 1 enterprise will get off the ground quickly, but it may not last.

If you want to be a pop-singer, choose a name for yourself or your group that adds sparkle—1, 3, or 5 might do the trick.

Fame, standing out in a crowd and being memorable is worth considering for any writer or entertainer, so a Number 1, 3, or 8 might work here.

If you want to be seen as lovable, choose 2 or 6.

Fancy a career as a healer, Tarot reader, or psychic? Choose Number 7 or perhaps 9.

If you are fed up with the wandering life and want to settle down, select a house with a number that adds up to 4.

If you are bored with being settled, move into a house with a number that adds up to 5.

A business related to design, architecture, building, surveying, and insurance is enhanced by a name that adds up to 22.

There are other ways around the problem; for instance, if you move into a house with the "wrong" number and this really bothers you, give your home a name that adds up to the "right" number for you.

As you can see, there are millions of variations on these themes, but, while it is fun to think this way, especially when choosing a name for a specific purpose, it wouldn't do to become obsessive about it; that is never a positive attitude, which is always the most important factor in life.

Key Letters

Sometimes your name number doesn't work out to be as strong as you would like, but that is saved by just looking at the first letter of your name. It has particular strength. Here are the letter and number combinations:

1	A, J, S
2	B, K, T
3	C, L, U
4	D, M, V
5	E, N, W
6	F, O, X
7	G, P, Y
8	H, Q, Z
9	I, R

Even if you can't choose a name that fits your criterion for some particular purpose, at least choose a good first letter. Anyone who has tried to get a book published knows how hard this is to pull off, but many of my successful writing friends have first names that begin with a Number 1. If you don't believe me, look at the other books in this *Plain and Simple* series: Anne, Jon, Sasha, Jacqueline, and then there is Cass and Janie—a husband and wife team. Janie has always been a writer, bit it is only after he ended a different career that her creative husband, Cass, joined her in writing. Leanna is as much an artist on the computer as a writer, so it is not surprising that her first letter is a creative one.

Gambling

Finally, numbers and the concept of money are inextricably linked. If you want to seriously study numerology, then unlink those two concepts!

If numerology could predict wins on horses, lotteries, roulette, card games or anything else, numerologists would be million-aires. Even though this book discusses predictive techniques, I do not recommend or endorse using numerology for any type of gambling.

Try another practical guide in the
ORION PLAIN AND SIMPLE
series

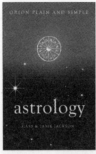

astrology

CASS & JANIE JACKSON

totem
animals

CELIA M DUNN

runes

KIM FARNELL

palmistry

SASHA FENTON

body
reading

SASHA FENTON

numerology

ANNE CHRISTIE

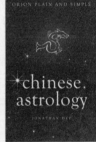

chinese
astrology

JONATHAN DEE

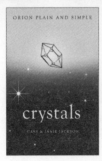

crystals

CASS & JANIE JACKSON

reincarnation

KRYS & JASS GODLY

angels

BELETA GREENAWAY